DISCOVER KILKENNY

JOHN BRADLEY

John Bradley is an archaeologist and a native of Kilkenny. He has directed excavations on a range of sites throughout Ireland, most notably a twenty-year research project on the *crannóg* of Moynagh Lough, County Meath. He has made a specialist study of Ireland's medieval towns and is the author of over seventy articles published in a wide variety of books and journals both at home and abroad. He is currently a senior lecturer in modern history at the National University of Ireland, Maynooth.

Discover KILKENNY

JOHN BRADLEY

THE O'BRIEN PRESS
DUBLIN

First published 2000 by The O'Brien Press Ltd.,
20 Victoria Road, Dublin 6, Ireland.
Tel. +353 1 4923333; Fax. +353 1 4922777
E-mail books@obrien.ie
Website www.obrien.ie

ISBN: 0-86278-661-4

British Library Cataloguing-in-Publication Data.
A catalogue record for this title is available from the British Library.

1 2 3 4 5 6 7 8 9 10
00 01 02 03 04 05 06 07

The O'Brien Press receives assistance from

The Arts Council
An Chomhairle Ealaíon

Layout and design: The O'Brien Press Ltd.
Maps: Design Image; Ivan O'Brien
Illustrations: Anne Farrall
Colour separations: C&A Print Services Ltd.
Printing: Zure S.A.

ACKNOWLEDGEMENTS

The author and publisher wish to thank the following for permission to reproduce visual material: Pat Nolan, Southeast Tourism Authority, pp.56, 74, 92, 94, 99, 101, 104 (bottom), 105, 107, 112 (bottom), Colour Section: pp.1 (bottom), 2, 3 (bottom), 6 (bottom), 11 (bottom), 12 (bottom), 13 (bottom), 14 (bottom), 15 (bottom), 16 (both); Oliver of Kilkenny, pp.119, 118, Colour Section: pp.1 (top), 3 (top), 4 (both), 5, 6 (top), 7, 8 (top), 9, 10, 11 (top), 12 (top), 13 (top), 14 (top), 15 (top) and front cover; Kilkenny Archaeological Society, pp.48, 53, 57, 61, 68, 72, 78, 115, 120, 122; John Kennedy and The Green Studio, pp.25, 30, 103, 109; Reproduction of painting on p.126 courtesy of The National Gallery of Ireland; Michael O'Brien, pp.10, 18, 23, 71, 88, 95, 113,117, 123; Anne Farrall for front and back cover illustrations (top) and b/w illustrations throughout. The author would like to extend special thanks to Mary Flood and Michael O'Dwyer at Rothe House; Donal O'Brien, Kilkenny Town Clerk; Paddy Friel and Proinsias Ó Drisceoil for their assistance with several important points of information; Michael Potterton and Patricia Ryan for their help with the text; and extra-special thanks to Rachel Pierce of The O'Brien Press for her dedication and resourcefulness.

For Tricia

CONTENTS

PART ONE: The History of the City

PART TWO: Guide to the Historic City

THE HISTORY OF THE CITY

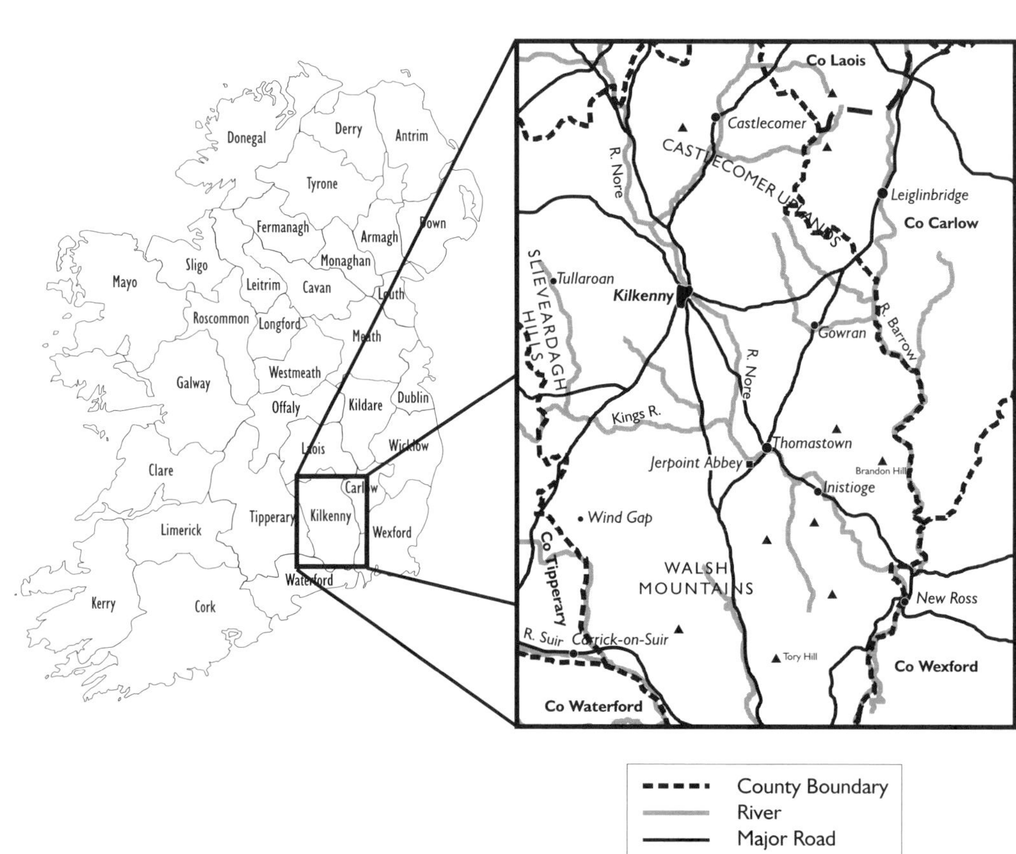

Map of Ireland and County Kilkenny.

Discover Kilkenny

Kilkenny retains more of its medieval character than any other Irish city, and visitors come in large numbers to explore its ancient buildings and to enjoy its distinctive townscape. In doing so they are themselves part of a long tradition, because from at least the 1580s travellers have been delighted by what they have found. The poet Edmund Spenser (c.1552–1599) visited on at least two occasions and wrote in the *Faerie Queene* of 'the stubborn Nore whose waters grey by fair Kilkenny and Rosponte [New Ross, County Wexford] board'. In the sixteenth century, the word 'fair' meant beautiful, as in the phrase 'the fair sex'. To this day the motto of Kilkenny is 'the faire citie'.

The survival of medieval Kilkenny, however, can be attributed more to accident than to design. Up until the 1650s the city played a much more significant role in Irish life than it does today, and it was only because later generations of townspeople could not afford to demolish the old buildings and build afresh that so much of the original city survived.

Tomb of Anastasia Tobyn, who died about 1405, St Patrick's churchyard.

The city lies on a bend of the River Nore and is the focal point of a small plain that forms the fertile heartland of County Kilkenny. This plain lies entirely within County Kilkenny, stretching eastwards and northwards as far as the Castlecomer Uplands, southwards until it reaches the Walsh Mountains, and westwards to the Slieveardagh Hills and the boggy zone that constitutes the border between counties Tipperary and Kilkenny. The plain is particularly obvious if one approaches the city from the west, along the old road from Cashel, County Tipperary, that passes through the Tullaroan Hills, about 12km from the city. But it can also be seen from the top of the round tower at St Canice's Cathedral or from the windows of Kilkenny Castle.

Origins

Kilkenny originated in the fifth or sixth century as an Early Christian settlement, and the Irish form of the place name, *Cill Chainnigh* ('Canice's Church'), indicates that its significance was at one time purely ecclesiastical. In fact, the church of Canice was not the first Christian foundation in the town. That distinction belongs to St Patrick's Church, represented today by a D-shaped graveyard in Patrick Street. First mentioned in the late seventh century as a *martartech* or house of relics, St Patrick's Church was by that time an old building, dating back to the earliest phase of Christianity in southern Ireland. The dedication of the church to Patrick may be as old as the seventh century, but the traditional view that the saint actually visited the site is no longer accepted.

The customary interpretation of the foundation of St Canice's Church is that the holy man arrived in person and established the site that commemorates his name. However, such an explanation is unlikely. Just as St Patrick's Cathedral in New York was not established by St Patrick, it is more likely, given what we know about Canice, that it was his followers or disciples who introduced his cult to the area. Canice's principal church was at Aghaboe in County Laois. Aghaboe, like Kilkenny, was within the territory of an ancient people known as the *Osraige* (literally 'deer people'), and their patron saint was Canice. During the sixth and seventh centuries, the tribal grouping that controlled Aghaboe emerged as the most powerful within *Osraige*. In due course this tribal grouping, the predecessors of the family later known as Mac Gilla Pátraic (anglicised as FitzPatrick), expanded their power into the Kilkenny area and introduced the cult of Canice. Throughout the first millennium, *Osraige* remained a buffer state,

St Canice's (Kenny's) Well. The seventeenth-century well-house is built over a site traditionally associated with St Canice, but it was almost certainly used in pre-Christian times. The remains of a Bronze Age cemetery have been found nearby. Water is still drawn from the well today; its taste is preferred to that of the city water supply.

caught between the ambitions of the rival kings of Leinster and Munster. Nonetheless, the *Osraige* managed to retain their independence from both provincial powers and when the Irish dioceses were organised on a territorial basis in 1111, the right of the *Osraige* to a separate bishop was recognised and the diocese of *Osraige* (anglicised as Ossory) was established.

Viking Age developments

Although the church of Canice has its origins in the late sixth or seventh century, it was not until the middle of the ninth century that the settlement became of more than local importance. In the 840s, a powerful and ambitious king named Cerball mac Dúnglainge (d. 888) emerged. His success was due in large measure to two abilities. Firstly, a skill in manipulating rival bands of Vikings by a combination of diplomacy and marriage alliances, and secondly, military prowess – he was able to defeat the Vikings in battle when necessary.

The Vikings came to Ireland initially as raiders, but by the 850s they had begun to settle down. Raiding remained important to them, but now their primary interest was to generate wealth for themselves. Wealth could be achieved by trade and also by making suitable marriage arrangements and political alliances. In fact, the presence of the Vikings in Ireland brought a new dimension to Irish waterways, so that the rivers Nore and Barrow, reaching some forty miles into the interior, became major arteries of communication.

Cerball's success was founded on his domination of the river valleys and, during the 870s and 880s, this made him the most powerful king in Leinster. Control of these waterways conferred the sort of wealth that the financiers of later ages would discover in railways, canals and roads. The relevance of Cerball mac Dúnglainge's rise to prominence lies in the fact that the fertile plain of central Kilkenny became one of the major power-centres in southeastern Ireland. This growth in power, which commenced in the late ninth century and was consolidated in the tenth and eleventh centuries, effectively marks Kilkenny's beginnings as a town.

Kilkenny on the eve of the Anglo-Norman invasion

The church dedicated to Canice was established on a hill overlooking the major fording-point of the River Nore, beside Green's Bridge. Nothing is known of the form of the early church, but examination of the modern street pattern suggests that it stood within a large enclosure, similar to that known from other large monasteries such as Armagh, Clonmacnoise, Kells and Kildare. The former existence of this enclosure is indicated by the curving alignment (best seen on a map) of Vicar Street, Dean Street and Thomas Street. It is thought that within the enclosure, following the normal Irish practice, there would have been a number of churches and oratories. The surviving round tower dates to the eleventh or early twelfth century and it was built on top of an earlier cemetery, containing the burials of both adults and children. Finds of bone and antler indicate that craftworking was also carried out.

St Canice's Cathedral, as it appeared in 1791.

By the twelfth century the Mac Gilla Pátraic kings of Ossory had a residence at Kilkenny in which they held court, and in which a deputy acted during their absence. The precise location of their residence, however, is unclear. It may have been within the ecclesiastical enclosure or, possibly, on the site of the later Kilkenny Castle. Archaeological excavations at the castle have revealed evidence for bronzeworking and ironworking associated with a sod building predating the initial Anglo-Norman earthwork castle. It is not known, however, if these activities were associated with a Mac Gilla Pátraic residence or not.

The arrival of the Anglo-Normans saw the formation of an area known as Hightown (or Englishtown), and St Canice's became the centre of a separate town, significantly called Irishtown. Even up to the late sixteenth century, the townspeople retained the tradition that Irishtown was the older settlement of the two, and it is in the persistent squabbling between the corporations of Irishtown and Hightown that the origin of the nickname 'Kilkenny cats' is to be found.

The Anglo-Norman town

By 1169, when the first Anglo-Normans visited the town and were put up in its inns or 'ostels', Kilkenny was already the largest and most important inland settlement in southeastern Ireland. The process by which the Anglo-Normans settled the modern county of Kilkenny is unclear in all its details, but it is evident that they had built an earthwork castle at Kilkenny by 1173 when it was burnt down by Donal Mór O'Brien, king of Limerick. The Anglo-Norman garrison was forced out and they do not appear to have renewed their interest in Kilkenny until the 1190s.

Kilkenny formed part of the lordship of Leinster, which was established by the leader of the Anglo-Norman adventurers, Richard FitzGilbert de Clare, better known as Strongbow. This lordship consisted of the modern counties of Dublin, Wicklow, Wexford, Kildare, Carlow, Kilkenny, Laois and parts of Offaly. As a result of the Anglo-Norman conquest, this large area was effectively Strongbow's private demesne. Strongbow died in 1176, leaving a daughter, Isabella, as his sole heir. As soon as Isabella came of age, in 1189, she was married to William Marshall, one of Henry II's staunchest supporters.

Marshall was a charismatic, dynamic and energetic figure, who devoted himself to managing the vast estates in Ireland, Wales, England and France, brought to

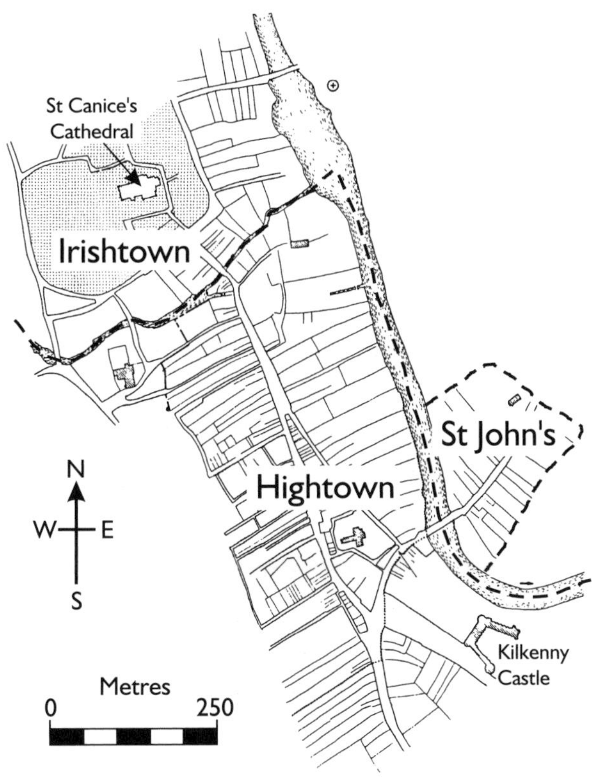

Irishtown, Hightown and the suburb of St John's, the principal areas of the medieval town.

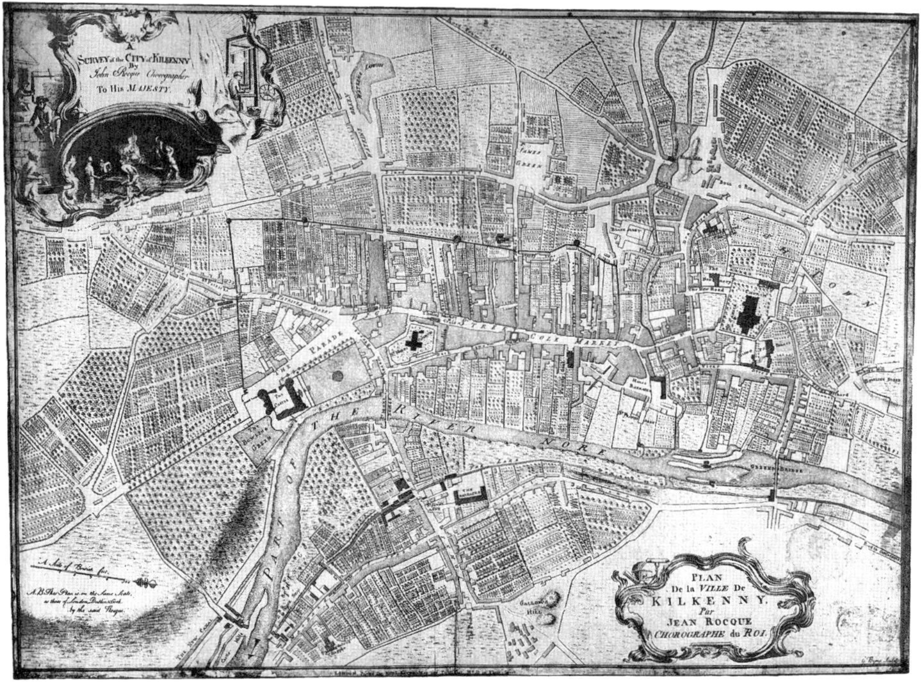

Jean Rocque's map of Kilkenny in 1758.

him as a result of marriage with Isabella. Henry II had retained control of Dublin, Wexford and Waterford – the major port towns of eastern Ireland – and with these denied to him, Marshall decided instead to establish two regional capitals in his Leinster lordship: Kildare in the north and Kilkenny in the south. Each 'capital' was to function as the principal market place of its region, and as the collection point from which animals and produce could be moved to Dublin or to the new port that Marshall had established at New Ross in County Wexford.

In 1207 there were sufficient inhabitants to warrant the issuing of a charter and, in the same year or shortly after, Marshall commenced the construction of what is now Kilkenny Castle. The castle was strategically placed overlooking a bridging-point of the River Nore, some 750m south of St Canice's Cathedral. The castle formed the southern boundary of the new Anglo-Norman settlement, Hightown, that was gradually built along a single north-south street, High Street, which stretched between the castle and the cathedral.

Regularly arranged plots, called burgage plots, were the backbone of the Anglo-Norman town plan. Until recently, many of the properties along High Street and Parliament Street (the relatively modern name of the northern end of the medieval High Street), preserved these long narrow plots, which are characteristic of medieval towns throughout western Europe. On each plot a townsman, known as a burgess, built a house for his family, usually with a shop on the street frontage, and behind the house there was space for outhouses, sheds, yards, gardens or orchards. In return for this plot of land, each burgess paid 1s. (one shilling) annually to the lord of the town, namely William Marshall and his successors. One shilling (5p today) does not sound like much, but in the early years of the thirteenth century its purchasing power was the equivalent of over £1,000 today. The charter of 1207 permitted the burgesses to draw timber from the Lord's Woods outside the town and it is likely that this provided the main building material for the initial houses.

Kilkenny also expanded to the east and south. An Augustinian monastery, St John's Abbey, was founded on the east bank of the River Nore about 1211 and a suburb, known simply as St John's, grew up in its vicinity (along the present John Street) during the thirteenth century. On the south side of the town, in the neighbourhood of St Patrick's Church, was the borough of Donaghmore, first referred to c.1250. The exact foundation date of the Hospital of St Mary Magdalen, which was situated in Maudlin (ie, Magdalen) Street, is unclear, but it was in existence by 1327 when it is first referred to. The entire settlement of Kilkenny was defended by a town wall, which was commenced about 1250 and slowly built over the next one hundred years. The population of the thirteenth-century town is thought to have ranged between 2,500 and 4,000 persons.

The remains of St John's Augustinian Priory in 1791.

Life in the medieval town, 1200–1540

Kilkenny is one of the few Irish centres with surviving medieval town records. The oldest corporation book is known as the *Liber Primus Kilkenniensis* (literally, 'Kilkenny's first book'). It commences with a record of 1230 granting permission to the townspeople to elect a council of twelve men and a town governor, who was to be called the sovereign of the town. This entry takes pride of place within the book because it marked the beginnings of formal urban government in the town and was a statement of the town's independence from the lord of the castle. The council and sovereign were the ancestors of the present-day mayor and corporation. This first document was written in French, which remained the principal language of Kilkenny until the fourteenth century and remained the official language of the courts and of government until the middle of the fifteenth century. The other main language was Latin, which, as an international tongue, was used for many ecclesiastical, legal and business agreements. The first English entries in the *Liber Primus Kilkenniensis* occur in 1448.

M[emorandum] that on Friday next before the feast of St. Michael the archangel A.D. 1230 (Sept. 27, 1230) it was ordained and established by assent of the community of Kilkenny that at every feast of St. Michael the archangel the said community should be assembled to elect their sovereign and the twelve (le doseyn) who are best and can govern and counsel their sovereign to the profit of the said community and are sworn to this.

Extract from the beginning of the *Liber Primus Kilkenniensis*.

From the *Liber Primus*, it is clear that the town was run by and for the burgesses – the property-owning citizens of the town. In the early thirteenth century, Kilkenny appears to have had 350 burgesses, but by 1384 this number had been reduced to 120. This reduction may reflect population decline, but it is more likely to represent the gradual restriction of burgess privileges to a smaller and smaller group of people. These privileges were designed primarily to protect the burgesses from arbitrary aristocratic or judicial pressures. The privileges included the right to trial before one's equals; the right to hold their own weekly court, known as the 'hundred court', and to set the level of its fines; the burgesses, their sons, daughters and widows were entitled to contract marriages without the permission of the lord; they could dispose of their burgages and personal possessions freely (except to members of religious orders); they were permitted to come and go freely; they were entitled to form a merchant guild to regulate their business; they could seize the goods of persistent debtors; and they could limit the trading licence of external merchants (specifically bakers and vintners) to forty days. Although to our eyes these privileges seem very ordinary, they were of huge importance in the thirteenth century, when ninety percent of the population was tied to the land and was bought and sold with it. Being a burgess meant the opportunity to create an independent life for oneself. Initially all of the burgesses were men, but by 1384 at least four women were listed as burgesses.

Status was conferred by office. To insult the sovereign's wife, for instance, was a much more serious offence than to insult a woman who happened to be a burgess or a burgess's wife. The holding of office, however, was expensive. Civic funds were negligible and the sovereign was normally expected to pay all of his expenses out of his own pocket. This automatically restricted the position to the richest citizens. There were laws regulating the wearing of clothes – furs and expensive robes could only be worn by people of high social status, and wealth on its own was insufficient to confer such standing. Status was also conferred by proximity to the landed aristocracy or to the Church. Intermarriage between a burgess and a member of the landed aristocracy was a social impossibility, but burgesses could gain status and amass wealth by serving as agents or administrators to the landed gentry. This prompted the burgesses to marry among themselves, and eventually the town's wealth accrued to a handful of prominent families.

The tomb of William and Margaret Goer at St Mary's churchyard provides a record of the costume worn by the burgesses of Kilkenny in the second half of the fourteenth century.

Ranking below the burgesses were free tenants. They too could own property and had most of the privileges of burgesses, but they could not take part in civic elections or become a member of the governing council. Below the free tenants were craftspeople, labourers, servants and others who rented dwellings within the town. They had none of the rights or privileges of burgesses and, although they might enjoy the freedom of the town, it would be expected, for instance, that they would seek their master's or employer's approval before marrying. Unfortunately, as is usual with many documents, they shed light only on the well-off sector of society, so there is little information about the lifestyles of the poor, who formed the majority of the town's population.

Kilkenny's primary importance at that time was as a market place for the fruits of the soil. The list of produce sold in the medieval market place included cereals (wheat, oats and barley), vegetables (peas and onions), fowl (hens and geese), bread and flour, dairy produce (butter, cheese and eggs), as well as exotic imported commodities such as salt, mustard, pepper, almonds, cummin, figs and raisins. Cattle, sheep, pigs and horses were sold at the fairs that were held three times per year, while the provision of stabling and fodder was a steady source of revenue for the townspeople. There was a trade in game birds, and in the skins of hunted animals such as fox, squirrel, badger, hare, rabbit and deer. Pigeons were kept as a source both of meat and eggs, although the number of dovecotes in the town seems to have been small. Fishing was an important source of food and fishermen lived, fished and traded in the town. There is evidence for the sale of salmon and eel, which could have been caught locally, as well as hake, herring and salted conger eel, which must have been imported from the coast, some fifty to sixty kilometres away.

The Market Slip.

The long gardens at the rear of the burgage plots enabled the burgesses to grow their own vegetables and herbs, as well as to plant orchards for apples, pears and other fruit. By the end of the fifteenth century, gardens within and without the town were extensively planted with madder, a lucrative crop that provided a colouring agent used for dyeing textiles. Use of the commonage, the land held in common by the burgesses, which stretched for two miles outside the walls, was strictly controlled. Digging was prohibited and tenants were required to keep the land 'playne [ie, open] and grene' so that it could be used for shooting and archery by the townspeople.

North of the town were woods, which, as late as the seventeenth century, produced oak timbers large enough for building purposes, while south of the town was the 'common quarry' (now the Black Quarry), from which burgesses were permitted to remove building stone freely. When polished, the stone from this quarry became black in colour, hence its later name. Although the stone from the quarry was limestone, it was almost always referred to by early writers as 'marble' and this gave rise to Kilkenny's nickname: 'the marble city'.

The town's hinterland consists of good grain-growing countryside and flour milling was an important part of the medieval economy. There were ten watermills in the immediate vicinity of the town. The control of milling could be lucrative and was vested in the lords of the town. William Marshall and his descendants owned six mills, which served Hightown, while the bishops of Ossory owned four mills in Irishtown.

All burgesses and freemen had the right to bake bread and brew ale; the number of individuals brewing ale in the town has been calculated at between 265 and 400. Most brewing was probably for domestic consumption, but alehouses were evidently popular. One of the local authority's principal concerns throughout the period was the standardisation of drinking measures in these alehouses to ensure that customers were treated fairly. A late fourteenth-century bill enumerates five alehouse owners, three of whom were women, while one was also in the business of supplying bread. Private brewing remained characteristic of the town until the seventeenth century, when the practice was curtailed in favour of commercial brewing. Wine taverns are mentioned in the 1207 charter, but the absence of any further specific mentions suggests that they were replaced by alehouses. Pottery from Saintonge, in southwestern France, has been found on several archaeological excavations in the town, indicating that much of the wine came from Bordeaux.

The blacksmith was a key figure in every medieval town and Kilkenny was no exception. The town forge is first mentioned in 1307 and, although it was initially part of the property of the lord of the town, ownership had passed to the townspeople by the early fifteenth century. The forge was located in the centre of Hightown – an unusual location because forges were a potential

The market cross of Kilkenny, as depicted in a now lost painting of about 1760.

fire hazard and their number and distribution were carefully regulated. Other occupations recorded in the medieval town include carpenters, stonecutters, masons, butchers, bakers, chandlers, tanners, glovers, shoemakers, weavers, fullers (who finished and cleansed cloth), dyers, tailors, girdlers (manufacturers of waist-belts and girdles), barbers and general merchants, and there are references also to jailers, barristers, chaplains and clerks.

The witchcraft trial of Alice Kyteler, 1324

Culturally, the thirteenth-century town reflected the Anglo-Norman world of Ireland, Britain and France. French was the language of government and law, Latin, the language of the church, and English, the language of business and of work. Burgesses with pretensions to gentility took care to have their gravestones inscribed in French and, as late as 1324, when Bishop Richard de Ledrede denounced Lady Alice Kyteler as a heretic and sorceress, he read the charges in French, Latin and English, so that their content might be understood by all.

The trial of Alice Kyteler is interesting because it shows that Kilkenny formed part of the wider cultural world of Western Europe. Historically, it is significant for several reasons. It was the first witchcraft trial in European history to treat the accused as members of an organised group of heretics, and the first to accuse a woman of having acquired the power of sorcery by means of sexual intercourse with a demon. It was also the first European trial to link witchcraft with heresy, thereby setting in motion the witchcraft craze that led to the execution of hundreds of thousands of northern Europeans in the sixteenth and seventeenth centuries.

Today, sorcery, witchcraft and heresy are of little more than passing interest to most, but in the fourteenth century they were regarded as hideous crimes. Heresy had much the same standing as terrorism today – it was seen as a direct challenge to those in power. The society of the time was one in which the Church presided over every activity, whether public or private. It officiated at baptism; it recited the last rites. The coronations of kings and emperors were conducted by its rituals. The fields were blessed annually to ensure their fertility. Bishops were not just clergymen, they were great landed lords as well. Intellectually, the Church provided an all-encompassing picture of the meaning, aim and goal of human life, knitting together the social strata of prince and pauper, townsman and peasant. Never again was the purpose of life so clearly defined. Never again were Church and State so inextricably mixed. To challenge the Church was to threaten the entire social order, so the heretic was viewed not just as a religious dissenter but also as a social agitator.

Lady Alice Kyteler appears to have been a clever, resourceful and independent-minded woman. She was married four times, which would appear to indicate that she had some personal attractions, and she was a member of an important Kilkenny family of bankers. Her husbands were all wealthy and prominent men and, while her own family background provided her with social position, her marriages increased both her wealth and her power. She appears to have borne only one child, William Outlaw, the son of her first marriage, and the charges of heresy specifically state that she favoured him in preference to the stepchildren of her other marriages.

In 1324, Alice Kyteler and five other women were accused of being heretical sorceresses. Because Alice was one of the wealthiest and most influential women in Kilkenny, the incident became a *cause célèbre*. Seven sensational charges were placed against her and her accomplices:

(1) That in order to obtain their wishes by sorcery, they denied the faith of Christ and of the Church totally for a month or a year, depending on the magnitude of what they desired. During this time they believed in nothing in which the Church believed. They neither adored the Body of Christ nor entered any church. They neither heard Mass nor made use of consecrated bread or holy water.

(2) They made sacrifices to 'son of Art', one of the inferior demons of hell, at a crossroads near the town, using live cocks that they dismembered and scattered there.

(3) They asked advice and sought responses from demons by means of their sorcery.

(4) They took the jurisdiction and authority of the Church into their own hands. It was alleged that at their nightly meetings they issued the sentence of excommunication against their own husbands. Using lighted wax candles, they named, spat on and cursed each part of their husband's bodies, from the sole of the foot to the crown of the head, extinguishing their candles at the end with the words: 'fi, fi, fi, Amen'. (The meaning of the word

'fi' is unclear – it may be a short form of the Latin 'fiat', meaning 'let it be'.)

(5) They made powders, ointments, potions and candles by boiling a stew above a fire of oak wood. This stew consisted of the guts and internal organs of sacrificed cocks, dead men's nails, spiders, disfigured black worms, herbs such as milfoil (yarrow), pubic hair, the brains and clothing of boys who had died before being baptised, the decapitated head of a thief and countless other detestable things. These potions were used to arouse love and hate, to cause death, to maim the bodies of believing Christians and to make the faces of women appear to have horns like goats.

(6) The sons and daughters of Alice's four husbands had commenced litigation against her at the bishop's court. They openly accused her of killing some of their fathers through sorcery, and of infatuating others to such a degree that they gave all their possessions to her and to her own son, William Outlaw, permanently impoverishing their own and the heirs of previous marriages. Her present husband, the knight Sir John le Poer, was reduced to such a state by these powders, potions and witchcraft that he was totally emaciated, his nails had fallen out and there was not a hair on any part of his body. With the support of a serving woman, he had forcibly removed the keys of chests from his wife and, on opening them, discovered a sack full of the horrible ingredients described above.

(7) Alice had a demon *incubus*, called 'son of Art' or sometimes 'Robin, son of Art', who had sexual intercourse with her. He came to her sometimes in the form of a cat, at other times as a shaggy black dog or as a black man with two companions, both of whom were stouter and taller than he was, and one of whom carried an iron rod in his hands. She had given herself and all her possessions to this demon *incubus*, and she had acknowledged that she had received all her wealth and everything that she possessed from him.

One of Alice's accomplices, Petronilla of Meath, later confessed that with her own eyes, in full daylight, she had seen Robin, son of Art, materialise in the form of three black men bearing iron rods in their hands and had watched the apparition, thus armed, having sexual intercourse with Alice. Indeed, she added that she had dried the place after their departure, using the bedcover to do so.

The Kyteler case had started inconspicuously. In March 1317, the bishopric of Ossory became vacant and the papacy appointed an English Franciscan, Richard de Ledrede, who was probably in his early forties at the time. In character he was ambitious, wilful and determined, and he brought a strong sense of duty and orthodoxy to his episcopate. He was consecrated in April by the pope, at Avignon in the south of France, and he made his way to Kilkenny, where he held a diocesan synod at St Canice's Cathedral in September 1317. The provisions of this synod indicate that he had a reformer's zeal: he prohibited his clergy from having wives or keeping mistresses (they had to either give them up or resign), he prevented the handing out of church revenues to laymen and he stipulated that all heretics must be excommunicated.

Kyteler's Inn, the house traditionally associated with Alice Kyteler.

The pursuit of heretics was enjoined on all pastors and success in detecting them was a well-recognised route to promotion. Jacques Fournier, bishop of Pamiers in France, was a contemporary, perhaps even an acquaintance of Ledrede's. Fournier was an avid pursuer of heretics and was so successful that he ended his days as Pope Benedict XII. Bishops who failed in their duty could themselves be burnt as heretics, as happened to the unfortunate Hughes Geraud, bishop of Cahors in France, in 1318. The hot beds of heresy were the south of France and east central Europe; Britain and Ireland were largely oblivious to these developments. Indeed, when Bishop de Ledrede began to pursue heretics in Kilkenny, he was dismissed by Arnold le Poer, who proudly proclaimed that 'heretics have never been found in the land of Ireland, rather it was accustomed to be called *insula sanctorum*, the island of saints'. As seneschal or chief official of Kilkenny, Arnold le Poer was the chief administrative officer for the absentee Dispenser family (William Marshall's heirs), who were then the lords of Kilkenny.

Proceedings against Alice began in earnest when Bishop de Ledrede requested the Chancellor of Ireland to arrest her because she had been accused of heresy and sorcery. The chancellor, however, was Roger Outlaw, a cousin of Alice Kyteler's first husband, and he urged the bishop to drop his case. De Ledrede persisted and summoned Alice to appear before his own court in Irishtown, but Alice ignored the summons. A second date was set but Alice, using her influence with Arnold le Poer, sensationally had the bishop arrested and he was committed to prison in Kilkenny Castle. It may have been hoped that a spell in prison would bring the bishop to his senses, but it had precisely the opposite effect. Unable to obtain satisfaction in his own court, the bishop decided to appeal directly to the seneschal's court at Kilkenny Castle. De Ledrede describes how he proceeded there with great ceremony, dressed in his pontificals, carrying a monstrance with the sacred host and accompanied by a group of Dominicans and Franciscans in solemn procession. The courtroom was thrown into consternation by the bishop's dramatic arrival. The judge, Arnold le Poer, ordered the bishop to be removed, but eventually gave way to the pressure of those in the hall and the bishop was led back. 'Take this vile English rustic with that rubbish in his hands to the bar where thieves are accustomed to stand,' ordered the judge; the bishop refused to move. From the floor of the hall he read out the papal decretals that required the secular authorities to pursue heretics. The judge replied: 'Go to the church with your decretals and preach there. You can expect no assistance from this court or from me.'

Foiled again, the bishop was at a loss for what to do, but as chance would have it, John Darcy, the Justiciar of Ireland – the country's chief judicial officer – passed through Kilkenny in July 1324 and de Ledrede succeeded in having the case brought before him. Alice and her accomplices were found guilty of the charges. Alice, however, managed to slip out of Kilkenny. Her son, William Outlaw, publicly renounced his heresy and promised to atone by providing monies for the repair of St Canice's roof. Petronilla of Meath refused to retract her statement of guilt. She had been whipped senseless on six occasions in order to obtain a confession and had evidently lost her mind in the process. For refusing to abjure her heresies she was paraded through the streets of Kilkenny and burnt alive at the stake (which was probably set up in High Street), on 2 November 1324. Friar Clyn, a contemporary chronicler, records that she was the first person ever to die for heresy in Ireland.

The whole case made Bishop de Ledrede very unpopular and in 1327 he was forced to flee Kilkenny. He took shelter at Avignon, returning only in 1349 when he once more started to seek out heretics. Indeed the most informative document as to the bishop's motives comes from the 1350s, when it was alleged that he had been trumping up charges against the decent, simple, faithful people of Kilkenny as a means of extorting money from them. De Ledrede survived the accusations, however, and died of old age in 1360.

The tomb of Bishop Richard de Ledrede (d.1360) in St Canice's Cathedral.

It is doubtful if the full facts of the Kyteler case will ever be known. The description of John le Poer's body as emaciated and devoid of body hair fits the symptoms of arsenic poisoning and, taken in conjunction with the allegation that Alice had killed her previous husbands, it may be that she was slowly murdering her current husband. The principal motive of her accusers – her dispossessed stepchildren – appears to have been envy. The property and wealth of heretics did not pass to their blood heirs but reverted to the family's next of kin. In Alice Kyteler's case, her property and wealth would have been inherited by John le Poer, her fourth husband – both Alice and her son, William Outlaw, would have been dispossessed. The sack full of 'horrible and detestable' ingredients was almost certainly planted to frame Alice and to provide a set of dramatic and controversial exhibits at the trial. Under torture, confessions are relatively easy to extract. Petronilla of Meath was evidently so shattered by her ordeal that she believed she had actually taken part in nightly covens and that she had seen three black men materialise in front of her eyes and have sexual intercourse with Alice.

The source of the charges themselves is not difficult to trace. Seventeen years previously, much the same charges had been placed against the Knights Templars, the most noble order of European chivalry, by Philip the Fair, king of France. The motive, again, was greed. It is now accepted that those charges were false, but at the time they were used to crush the Templars. In 1309, as a result of the charges, the Templar house in Kilkenny was taken into the king's possession and the whole incident would have been a talking point all over the town.

Given such a background, the charges placed against Alice Kyteler would have fallen on fertile ground. William de Baskerville, the hero-detective of Umberto Eco's novel *The Name of the Rose*, says that he witnessed the trial of Alice Kyteler before leaving for Italy, where, in the course of the novel, he seeks to rescue the innocent by exposing the false methods of the medieval Inquisition. William de Baskerville, however, is a fictional character, and it is to be regretted that his methods of deductive reasoning did not exist in the fourteenth century. If they had, the Templars would not have been suppressed and Alice Kyteler would never have been put on trial.

The Black Death, 1348–1349

In general, the fourteenth century was a period of economic recession in Kilkenny. The town escaped the worst depredations of the Bruce Wars (1315–1318), but it is unlikely that it emerged untouched by the famines of 1315–1317, the smallpox epidemics of the 1320s, and the cattle plagues of 1321 and 1324–1325. The severest epidemic, however, was undoubtedly the Black Death – the bubonic plague that spread from Asia to Europe and was carried by fleas that preyed on rats and humans alike. It arrived in Kilkenny in 1348 and was graphically described by the Franciscan, Friar Clyn:

> The plague was so contagious that whoever touched the dead or the sick was immediately infected and died, and so both penitent and confessor were led to the grave. And because of fear and terror, men scarcely dared to perform the works of piety and mercy, namely, visiting the sick or burying the dead. Many died of boils and abscesses, and pustules on their shins or under their armpits; others died frantic with headache, and others spitting blood ... The pestilence grew strongest in Kilkenny during Lent, and between Christmas Day [1348] and March 6th [1349] eight friars preachers [Dominicans] died. Scarcely one person alone ever died in a house, but usually husband and wife with their children and household went the same way, that of death. And I, Friar John Clyn, of the Order of Friars Minor at Kilkenny, wrote in this book those notable things which happened in my time ... I leave parchment for continuing the work, if any man should survive, and any of the race of Adam escape this pestilence and continue the work that I have commenced.

The manuscript ends at this point and we may conclude that Friar Clyn, the major chronicler of local affairs, was another victim of the Black Death. So many people died there were labour shortages. Servants and labourers sought to exploit their scarcity value. The suburbs were deserted, chapels that had been built outside the walls were demolished and some properties within the town remained vacant for fifty years.

The remains of the Franciscan Friary, as drawn by Francis Grose in 1791.

In the countryside around Kilkenny, depopulation occurred mainly in the Anglo-Norman-held lands. The Gaelic Irish population was largely unaffected because the Anglo-Norman invaders had confined them to remote uplands and marginal land, but now they gradually returned to occupy the depopulated lands. Eventually, all of the land between Gowran (the eastern boundary of County Kilkenny) and Carlow fell into the hands of two Gaelic Irish families: the O'Nolans and the MacMurroughs. By the end of the fourteenth century, they had cut off the overland routes between Kilkenny and Dublin.

The Statute of Kilkenny, 1366

Kilkenny was a favoured venue for meetings of parliament and king's council (the medieval cabinet), one or other of which gathered in the town on at least thirty-four occasions between 1277 and 1425. Such assemblies were an important source of revenue for the local economy. The most famous (or infamous) of these meetings was the parliament of 1366, presided over by King Edward III's son, Lionel, duke of Clarence, which promulgated the 'Statute of Kilkenny'. This outlawed both intermarriage with the Gaelic Irish and the maintenance of a mistress of Gaelic Irish origin. It banned the practice of fosterage and prohibited the use of the Irish language and Irish law. It regulated trade with the Gaelic Irish, permitting traffic in meat during time of peace, but making the trade in horses, weapons and armour a treasonable offence. Individuals of Gaelic Irish birth were forbidden to join cathedral chapters, collegiate churches or religious houses. Hurling, riding without a saddle and Irish modes of dress were not permitted, while pipers, storytellers, 'babblers and rhymers' of

Gaelic Irish origin were neither to be admitted nor entertained. Finally, the maintenance of kerns (Irish mercenaries) or hobblers (Irish cavalry) during peacetime was outlawed.

The harshness of these provisions indicates a society under siege. Kilkenny in the 1360s saw itself as lying on the frontier between European civilisation (the Statute of Kilkenny was written in French) and the perceived barbarism of the Gaelic Irish way of life. In such situations, it has been observed that the colonist is gradually mastered by the frontier. Far from the civilised centre to which the colonist believes he belongs, the frontier forces him to adopt native practices (such as clothes, fosterage and entertainment) and intermarry with the native women in order to survive. This dilution of his ideals breeds a resentment of 'going native' that the colonist seeks to legislate against.

There is little evidence of any social interaction with the Gaelic Irish in the fourteenth-century town. The urban culture of the thirteenth and fourteenth centuries remained vehemently hostile to the Gaelic Irish and viewed them as 'natural enemies'. It is typified by the case of 1344, in which a Kilkenny judge ruled that because Adam Omolgan was an Irishman, his murder within the town did not have to be punished. The harshness of these attitudes appears to have lessened somewhat by the late fifteenth century, when burgesses and craftsmen with Gaelic Irish names are found in Kilkenny.

A key factor in this Gaelicisation of Kilkenny society may have been the purchase of the town by James Butler, the third earl of Ormond, in 1391. This broke the contact with English-based lords and brought in a family that had built up a power-base by the skilful management of the Gaelic Irish in the marches of Wicklow and Tipperary. The earl was a fluent Irish speaker and one of his first acts on arriving in Kilkenny was to contravene the Statute of Kilkenny by imposing the maintenance of his kerns for twelve weeks on the town. Within a year kerns were living within the town, much to the distress of some sections of the population.

The Butler family

James Butler was the first member of the Butler family to live in Kilkenny Castle, the family residence until the twentieth century. He purchased it, together with a great part of County Kilkenny, from the

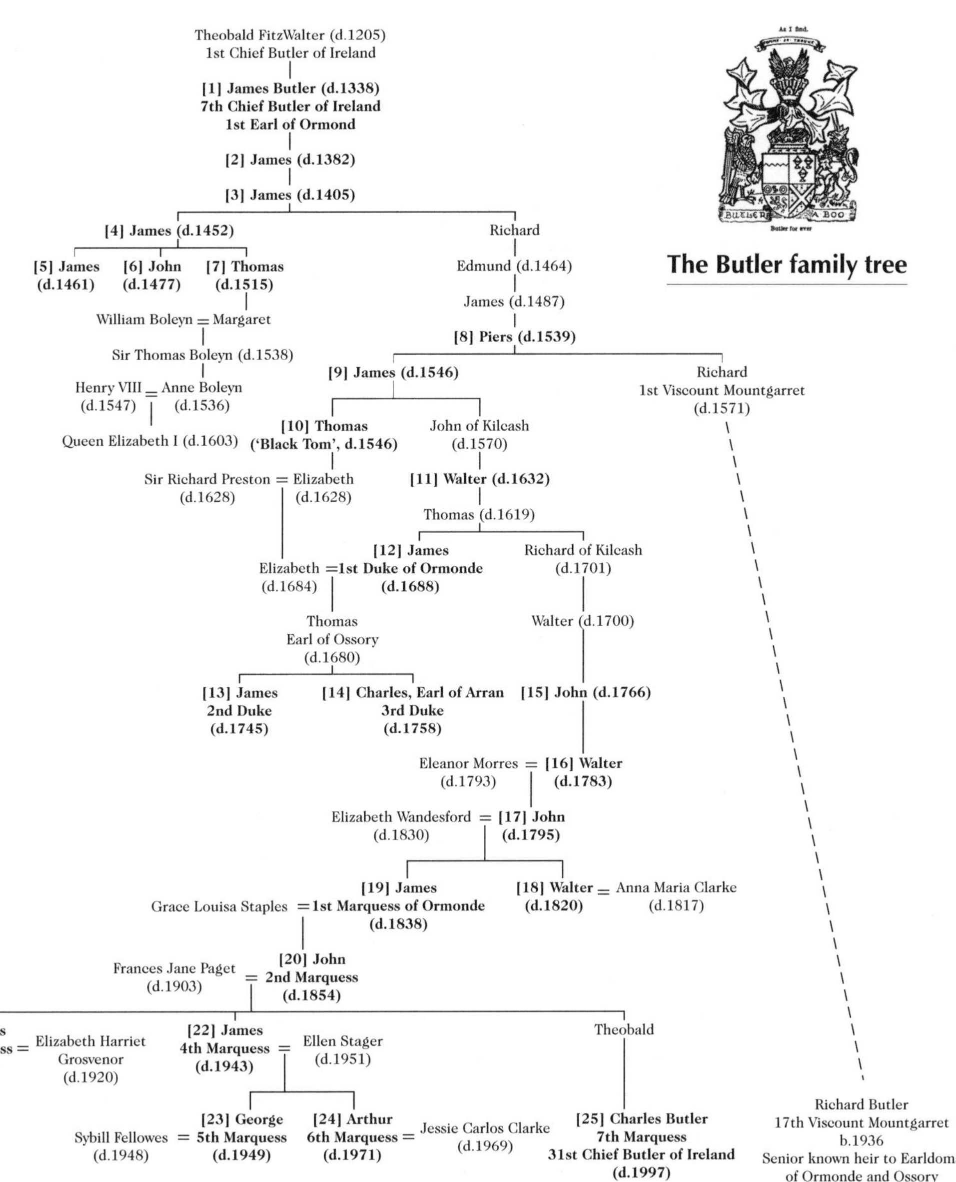

The Butler family tree

Dispenser family (William Marshall's heirs) in 1391 for the sum of £700. At a time when £1 would have purchased 4,000 pints of beer, this figure translates roughly into £30 million in today's money – so even then it was a bargain.

The Butler family – earls, marquesses and dukes of Ormond – came to Ireland with Prince John, son of Henry II, in 1185. They received large grants of land in County Tipperary, known then by its Irish name of *Oir Mhumhan* (literally, 'east Munster'), from which

Tombs at St Mary's Church, Gowran, County Kilkenny, thought to be those of James Butler (d.1338), first earl of Ormond, and his wife, Eleanor de Bohun (d.1363).

are derived the anglicised forms of Ormond or Ormonde – it was spelt without a terminal 'e' until 1642.

The family name, like many in the Middle Ages, stemmed from an occupation. The founder of the family was Theobald FitzWalter (d.1205), who was appointed the first chief butler of Ireland in, or shortly after, 1185. As chief butlers, they were butlers to the Crown, responsible for ensuring that whenever the king and his court were in Ireland they were provided with adequate supplies of food and alcohol. To facilitate them in this task, the Butlers were granted a special privilege known as the Prisage of Wine. This was the right to two out of every thirteen tuns of wine imported into the country (a tun is a wine cask holding 216 gallons), roughly the equivalent of fifteen percent of all wine. From the thirteenth until the fifteenth century, wine was perhaps the principal commodity imported into Ireland and, needless to say, the portion that the family received made them very rich and on occasion, no doubt, very merry as well. In 1811 the Crown bought back the right to the Prisage of Wine for £216,000 (about £250 million today) and much of the money was used to remodel and refurbish the castle.

From the seventeenth century onwards, many members of the family emigrated to Europe and America (the first attested Irishman in America, arriving in 1584, was Richard Butler). Many served in Continental armies and were ennobled for their services. Variations of the family name can be traced all over the world. In Spain and Sweden, they retained the name Butler, in France, they became Boutler or de Butler, in Austria and Germany, they became von Buttlar, and in Russia, they were known as Butleroff. In 1965 the Butler Society was established at Kilkenny Castle with the aim of forging contacts between the scattered branches of the family, and it now has members from all over the world. (For further information on the society's activities, visit their website at www.butler-soc.org)

Late Medieval Kilkenny, 1400–1540

Throughout the fifteenth century the town was isolated from the royal administration in Dublin by the Gaelic Irish, but it still remained as a functioning urban community. It was a period of urban consolidation, characterised by redevelopment and rebuilding within the town. There is evidence of a demand for building space within the walls, but no sign of suburban expansion. During the second half of the century, both major bridges (Green's Bridge and St John's Bridge) and almost all of the town gates, wall-towers, churches and religious houses were modified or rebuilt.

During the first half of the fifteenth century the earls of Ormond exerted a powerful local influence, but this declined after 1452, when the political ambitions of the Ormonds prompted them to take up residence in England. The fifth earl, James, was executed in 1461 after fighting on the Lancastrian side at the Battle of Towton in Yorkshire. His brothers, John, the sixth earl (1461–1477) and Thomas, the seventh earl (1477–1515), preferred to live on their Wiltshire estates, but the death of Thomas without male heirs occasioned a family crisis that led to the separation of the English and Irish lands.

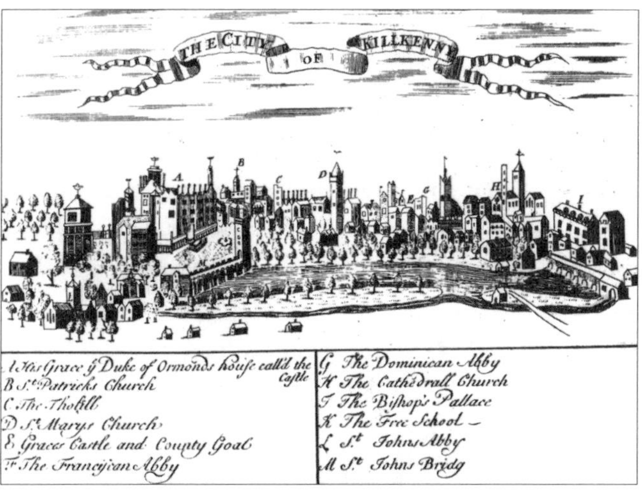

View of Kilkenny in 1704 by the map-maker Henry Pratt.

Much of the Wiltshire property eventually passed to the seventh earl's grandson, Sir Thomas Boleyn, better known as the father of Anne Boleyn and grandfather of Elizabeth I. In Ireland, however, the Butler lands were claimed by Piers Butler, a direct descendant of the third earl, and in 1538, after the Boleyns had fallen from favour, he succeeded in having himself recognised as eighth earl of Ormond.

Piers's cultural background combined both Gaelic Irish and Anglo-Irish strains and he was adept at making the best of both worlds. He established a grammar school in Kilkenny that, under the tutelage of Peter White, was to become one of Ireland's most famous colleges. Piers is also credited with importing Flemish weavers to make elaborate tapestries, carpets and cushions for Kilkenny Castle. In addition, however, he levied the customary rights of Gaelic lords on his Anglo-Irish subjects, who deeply resented it. In an inquisition, or public enquiry, of 1537 he was named as the lord of the town of Kilkenny, entitled to all of its chief rent, which amounted to IR£18, but he was also denounced by the corporation for the exactions, in the form of taxes and services, which he had imposed upon them. While the services exacted by the earl may have been demanding, the outspoken condemnation of their lord by the corporation indicates that it had become accustomed to a certain independence during the half century of Butler absence.

This incipient independence was linked to the development, from the late fifteenth century onwards, of a small exclusive ruling class, consisting of about fifteen families, that controlled the town until 1650. The names of ten were grouped together in a well-known couplet:

> **Archdekin, Archer, Cowley, Langton, Lee,**
> **Knaresborough, Lawless, Ragget, Rothe and Shee.**

There were other influential families also, the Hacketts, Walshes, Sherlocks and Savages among them, and together with the previous ten they controlled every civil and ecclesiastical position within the town. Some families were conspicuously prominent in public life. A member of the Rothe family, for instance, was appointed sovereign on eighteen occasions between 1440 and 1544; the Archers held the position sixteen times between 1434 and 1544; the Shees were sovereigns on seven occasions between 1493 and 1544. The control of these three families increased in the early sixteenth century, and between 1494 and 1544 only eighteen of the fifty sovereigns were neither Archers nor Rothes nor Shees. Dynastic supremacy was perpetuated by interfamilial marriages, and when the Dissolution of the Monasteries brought new land onto the market these families were excellently poised to take advantage of the speculative opportunities it afforded.

Reformation and Counter-Reformation, 1541–1615

The Dissolution of the Monasteries occurred as part of the Reformation, which broke the link with Rome and established King Henry VIII as head of both the Church of England and the Church of Ireland. The Act of Dissolution was rejected by the institutional Catholic Church, but individual burgesses of Kilkenny (all still devoutly Catholic) saw it as a golden opportunity to increase their wealth.

The remains of the Dominican Friary ('Black Abbey') in 1791.

In 1539 the sovereign and burgesses wrote to Thomas Cromwell, the lord great chamberlain of England, asking that they might be granted St Francis's Friary, the Black Abbey and the Hospital of St Mary Magdalen. Their request was granted in 1543. The acquisition of this new land made possible the first suburban development in Kilkenny for over two hundred years. During the second half of the sixteenth century rows of new houses were built on lands formerly belonging to the religious houses, particularly in Maudlin Street and Blackmill Street.

Apart from the reallocation of church lands in the 1540s, the Reformation appears to have had relatively little impact in Kilkenny until the 1570s and 1580s. This was due, in large measure, to the absence of both an active policy of reform and of competent ministers to carry it out. The Protestant parish churches were short-staffed and some, if not all, fell into disrepair.

The most famous exponent of the Reformation was John Bale (1495–1563), bishop of Ossory, a distinguished English cleric, best

Steps from Rose Inn Street to St Mary's Church.

remembered now as one of the founders of the study of English literature. He took up residence as bishop of Ossory in 1553. 'Bilious Bale', as he was called by his opponents, was a powerful preacher and a prolific propagandist for his own vision of Protestantism. In the six months that he spent at Kilkenny, he infuriated his clergy, antagonised his superiors and outraged traditionalists among the burgesses of the town. Bale introduced the 1552 version of the *Book of Common Prayer*, he replaced the splendour of vestments with the simplicity of a black gown and he cleared the cathedral of images and statues. His freshness, or perhaps his shock value, appealed to the younger generation. Bale wrote Biblical dramas as counter-blasts to the conventional *Corpus Christi* mystery plays, and in the summer of 1553 the young men of the town performed these dramas at the market cross. His zeal, coupled with his denunciations of dissolute clergy and dissipated administrators, aroused local opposition and shortly after the accession of the Catholic Queen Mary, he was forced to abandon Kilkenny in favour of Calvinist Geneva in Switzerland.

In 1570, when the pope excommunicated Mary's successor, Queen Elizabeth I, the public practice of Catholicism was forced underground. Nonetheless, by the close of the sixteenth century energetic Counter-Reformation priests, many of them members of the old civic families, had begun to minister in the town, sometimes openly but more often privately.

On the accession of James I in 1603, the Dominicans seized the Black Abbey and restored it for Catholic worship; the parish churches of St Patrick and St Mary were also repossessed and for a time it was thought that James I, as the son of Mary, Queen of Scots, might reinstate Catholicism. Such beliefs proved illusory, but it took a year, during which the Dublin government had to step in and imprison the (Catholic) sovereign, before the churches returned to Protestant use. This demonstrated that while the practice of Catholicism was prohibited, it commanded a huge popular following in the town, and during the early seventeenth century it continued to grow. By 1608, when the Jesuits had established themselves, there were sixteen Catholic priests in the town and by 1613 the number had increased to twenty-seven. By contrast, in 1615 only four Church of Ireland ministers, including the bishop and dean of Ossory, officiated in the town.

Renaissance influences, 1565–1620

The survival and revival of Catholicism in the late sixteenth and early seventeenth centuries was due largely to the protection it received from one of Ireland's most powerful political figures: Thomas Butler, tenth earl of Ormond, better known as Black Tom. He succeeded to the title as a young boy in 1546, and died almost seventy years later in 1614. A cousin of Queen Elizabeth and educated at court, he was an important patron of the arts and architecture. He was one of the dedicatees of Spenser's *Faerie Queene,* and the addressee of several Irish poems. He also introduced English Renaissance building styles to the southeast – the mansions that he constructed at Kilkenny Castle and at Carrick-on-Suir in the 1560s provided the inspiration for the smaller-scale housing of the urban merchant class. The remains of about ten such houses survive and depictions of others are known. Rothe House, built between 1594 and 1610, is the best-known and provides an almost unique insight into the living conditions of the wealthy urban middle class at this time.

Rothe House, a Tudor merchant's house built in 1594.

Houses such as Rothe House were a feature of the late sixteenth- and early seventeenth-century town. At ground level they had an arcaded stone walkway, substituted in places by wooden pentices or lean-tos, which served to link the separate house frontages and to create a covered passage, similar to the Rows at Chester. A visitor to Kilkenny in 1613 described the presence of about forty houses 'of grey marble [ie, limestone] most of them supported by pillars', while in 1620, Luke Gernon commented that:

> The houses are of grey marble fayrely builte, the fronts of theyr houses are supported (most of them) with pillars, or arches under which there is an open pavement to walke on.

Today the only surviving fragments of this type of arcaded walkway are at Rothe House and beside the Butter Slip.

The Dissolution of the Monasteries impacted on the poor because some of the religious houses had had hospitals where, in addition to treating the sick, they also looked after the old and infirm. The Hospital of St Mary Magdalen appears to have continued in use, albeit deprived of its lands, because it was, in effect, a retirement home for elderly burgesses, but there was no place to accommodate the destitute. In 1582, Sir Richard Shee established an almshouse for six 'honest, poor, unmarried men' and six widows of fifty years of age or more. In 1614, Thomas Butler left money to establish an almshouse in High Street, the Hospital of Our Blessed Saviour, later known as the Ormonde Poorhouse. His descendants moved the poorhouse to St John's Green in 1839, and it remained in use until the 1980s. It is now the home of the Samaritan movement in Kilkenny.

Shee Almshouse, built in 1582 by Richard Shee.

City charter, 1609

From at least the 1580s the burgesses made representations to the Crown that Kilkenny should be raised to the dignity of a city, and in 1609 it was accorded this status by James I. The city was declared to consist of both Irishtown and Hightown, although the corporations were to remain separate. The first officer was to be styled a mayor, and the council was to consist of eighteen aldermen. The first mayor was Robert Rothe and thirteen of the aldermen were either Archers, Rothes or Shees. The charter also listed the thirty-six members of the merchant staple, who controlled the city's trade, all but fifteen of whom were Archers, Rothes or Shees, demonstrating yet again the political dominance of those families.

There were deep antagonisms in seventeenth-century Ireland between the various ethnic groupings living on the island. These consisted of the Gaelic Irish (descendants of the pre-Anglo-Norman inhabitants), the Old English (descendants of the Anglo-Norman colonists) and the New English (settlers who had moved to Ireland since about 1550). The ruling families of Kilkenny were almost all Catholic and were naturally part of the Old English grouping. They were loyal to the Crown, but were worried that the Crown no longer valued their allegiance because of the presumption that all Catholics were agents, or potential agents, of England's principal enemies: France, Spain and the Papal States. As long as there was a powerful Protestant earl of Ormond to protect their interests these fears were remote, but uncertainty increased after the death of the tenth earl, Thomas, in 1614. His heir was his recently widowed daughter, Elizabeth. The Ormond property was eventually settled on her and a marriage was arranged with one of James I's Scottish favourites, Richard Preston, Lord Dingwall. The Ormond title and little else was inherited by the earl's Catholic nephew, Walter, who was imprisoned for eight years because of his refusal to accept this settlement.

In general, the twenty-five years between 1614 and 1639 were years of religious tolerance. David Rothe (1573–1650), appointed Catholic bishop of Ossory in 1618, resided openly in the city and in the course of his episcopate he organised a functioning diocese with a functioning parish system. The city was always keen to demonstrate, however, that while it might be Catholic, it was loyal. This is evident, for instance, in the deference and civic ritual with which the lord deputy (the chief governor of Ireland), Thomas, Viscount Wentworth, was received in 1637. Wentworth was to have a lasting local importance because he promoted the career of the twelfth earl of Ormonde, James Butler. Butler had been educated at court, he was a prominent Anglican and he had reunited the Ormonde title with the Ormonde lands by marrying his cousin, Elizabeth Preston. With the exception of ten years spent in exile with Charles II in France, James Butler played a key role in Irish politics from the day he succeeded to the earldom in 1632, until his death in 1688.

In 1642 the Old English became the reluctant allies of the Gaelic Irish due to the success of a rising in Ulster the year before. This rebellion, led by the Ulster gentry, had swept through the planted counties of Ulster and had specifically targeted English Protestant settlers. Possibly as many as 3,000 colonists were killed, while many more were humiliated, tortured and forced to flee. Ulster had been the most Protestant of the Irish provinces, but now, with the success of the rebellion, Protestants were confined to the coastal areas, and with the exception of some towns and forts the whole interior of Ireland came under Catholic control. The outrage felt by the Dublin government and, particularly, by the increasingly powerful parliament in London, necessitated the defence of English and Protestant interests in Ireland. Parliament's reaction was to group all Catholics together, whether rebel or loyal, Gaelic Irish or Old English, and label them as the common enemy.

The Dublin administration's immediate reaction was vindictive. It imprisoned and tortured several prominent members of the Old English gentry, shocking Irish Catholic opinion and forcing the Old English into making an accommodation with the Ulster rebels. The government's actions, however, were motivated as much by potential gain as by reactionary anger. Every previous revolt had been followed by the confiscation of lands, and the widespread extent of the 1641 rebellion meant that huge estates would come into the government's hands once they had suppressed the rebels. In March 1642 the English parliament forced Charles I to sign the Adventurers' Act, which used the prospect of confiscated Irish lands as the security on which to raise loans to send forces to Ireland to put down the rebellion. Significantly, the act also prohibited the king from granting pardons to the rebels without the consent of parliament. It was a consent that parliament had no intention of giving.

The Confederation of Kilkenny, 1642–1649

In May 1642 a national congregation of the Catholic clergy, joined by the leading nobility and gentry, met at Kilkenny, probably because of the prestige that Bishop Rothe enjoyed. The congregation gave ecclesiastical approval to the Ulster rising and called for the setting up of a provisional government of Ireland, under a supreme council. This was to be achieved by summoning a general assembly of confederate Catholics, representing parliamentary constituencies throughout Ireland. They called themselves confederates because it was a coming together of Old English, Gaelic Irish and some New English Catholics. Kilkenny, as the country's largest inland town, with spacious housing and lodging, was an obvious choice for the general assembly that convened in October 1642. It was the king's absolute right to summon parliament as and when he wished, and since he had not summoned the gathering that met at Kilkenny, its leaders maintained that it was an assembly rather than a parliament. In practice, however, the assembly had all of the trappings of a sovereign government and it was certainly viewed as a parliament both at home and abroad.

Aware of the developing rebellious situation in Britain, where parliament was about to go to war with Charles I, the confederates declared their loyalty to the Crown. In order to gain international support, they portrayed the movement not as a revolt but as a crusade to achieve religious freedoms. They sought the restoration of the privileges and rights of the Catholic Church as they had been prior to the Reformation, and, in an effort to heal divisions within their ranks, they required all Catholics to take an Oath of Association, affirming loyalty to God, king and country. The confederates sought secure title to their own properties, appointments to public office and government administration, Catholic control of parliament, limitations on the terms of office of chief governors and the right to establish Inns of Court, universities and common schools. These Catholic grievances were long-standing, but they ran completely counter to government policy, and with the outbreak of civil war in England, the most that the king could do was equivocate.

The altered remains of the Shee house, which was used in 1642 for the first meeting of the Confederation of Kilkenny, as recorded in *Hall's Ireland* in 1842.

The confederates quickly realised that a parliamentary victory in the English Civil War would entail a new conquest of Ireland and the confiscation of their estates, so they sought a rapid compromise settlement with the king. The assembly endeavoured to allay Protestant fears, and perhaps gain Protestant support, by affirming that land ownership would have to be restored to the way it had been before the rebellion. The assembly also issued ordinances protecting Protestant-owned property and prohibiting assaults on Protestants.

The reality on the ground was different, however, as unruly mobs took the law into their own hands and vented their resentment. Houses, both of Catholics and Protestants alike, were looted in Kilkenny, churches were desecrated and, although no Protestants were killed, many were intimidated into abandoning their homes, while others were stripped naked, forced to run through the streets and abused. Most found refuge in Kilkenny Castle, from where the countess of Ormonde, Elizabeth Butler (née Preston), escorted them to Carrick-on-Suir, County Tipperary, and arranged safe passage to Waterford. Looting only seems to have stopped when Richard Butler, Lord Mountgarret, commander of the armed forces in the town and the future president of the supreme council, intercepted a member of the local gentry in the process of looting and shot him dead.

Despite the demands of extremists within the assembly, such as the archbishop of Cashel, who called for the execution of all Protestants, looting and intimidation served only to embarrass the confederate government. A similar unease affected Bishop Rothe, who was reluctant to occupy the Bishop's Palace and St Canice's Cathedral, knowing that it would send out all the wrong signals both to Charles I and to the English parliament. It would indicate that the Catholics wished to deprive the State of its powers and to determine themselves who should and who should not control the diocese of Ossory. In the jubilant mood of Catholic triumph, however, Bishop Rothe was persuaded to rededicate the church and to take possession of the revenues and properties of the see. There was a Catholic renaissance during the following years, reflected artistically in the quality of the stone tombs erected between 1642 and 1649 at St Mary's Church and at St Canice's Cathedral. The old parish churches, many of which were in disrepair, were rebuilt, the Dominicans regained their old friary (the Black Abbey), the Capuchins established a new one, the Jesuits founded a college and a novitiate, the Franciscans opened a nunnery and Bishop Rothe established a Catholic college at Rose Inn Street.

The city prospered during the Confederation period. A French traveller, François de la Boullaye le Gouz, who visited Kilkenny in 1644, found that every hotel and lodging house was full. His account provides an outsider's view of Kilkenny at this time and highlights the distrust of foreigners that was a necessary feature of the rebel capital:

> The city is the size of Orleans, seated on a small river that empties itself into the sea at eighteen miles distance. The castle is placed on the river. There are monasteries of Jacobins [Dominicans], of Recolets [Franciscans], and a college of Jesuits, who are held

> in great honour among the people. At the gates of the city they seized upon me and led me to the mayor, who judging by my physiognomy that I was English, told me that I was a spy – that my figure, my speech, and carriage were those of a native of England. I maintained that he was mistaken, and as politely as I could contradicted him telling him I was of the French nation and a good Catholic; that the passports I had from the king of England were proof of what I advanced, that he might read them and inform himself of my profession. He took them rudely enough from my hands, and reading only the superscription in English *Mestre le Gouz, his passe*, he was confirmed in his error, and said to the company: 'See, if this name be not English, and if I have not judged rightly that this fellow is a spy. Let the soldiers come and take him to prison; we do not so easily suffer these sort of ramblers; we will soon discover the truth'. The impertinence of the mayor shocked me. I replied to him 'You say I am English without any foundation but your imagination. Is there no Frenchman here who can judge if the French language is not natural to me, and English strange? As for my name, it is English; and it may be that my ancestors formerly came from England to live in Brittany, after the invasion of the Saxons, as those of many other French families did'. He sent in search of an inhabitant, a native of Caen in Normandy, who assured him that I was French. I had leave to withdraw and owing to the Catholic Council which was held in this town the hotels were so full, that if I had not met with a Norman called Beauregard, I should have been forced to lie in the streets.

Perhaps the most distinguished visitor to the city at this time was Giovanni Battista Rinuccini (d.1665), archbishop of Fermo, ambassador of the Papal States, who arrived at Kilkenny in 1645. Since his presence represented international approval of the Confederation, Rinuccini was received with all the pomp that the city could muster. As he approached Kilkenny, carried on a litter, he was met by a deputation of the local gentry and a group of fifty scholars, who welcomed him with a specially composed set of verses. The clergy lined up to greet him outside St Patrick's Church and processed in front of him as far as St Patrick's Gate, where he was formally welcomed by the corporation. Rinuccini continues his account:

> I then mounted on horseback wearing the pontifical cape and hat; the poles of my canopy were carried by some of the citizens who walked uncovered though it was raining. All the way to the cathedral, a distance perhaps not less than the length of the Via Lungara in Rome, was lined with soldiers on foot carrying muskets. In the middle of the city and at the foot of a high cross [the market cross], where a crowd was also assembled, we all stopped and a youth pronounced an oration, after which we moved on till we reached the church [St Canice's Cathedral]. Here, at the door, the bishop of Ossory [David Rothe], although of great age met me in the cope [a formal vestment worn on solemn occasions], offered me the aspersorium [vessel of holy water] and incense, and conducting me to the high altar delivered an address suitable to the ceremony, after which I gave a solemn benediction and granted the indulgences, and then another oration was pronounced in honour of my arrival.

Rinuccini's mission was to restore the public worship of Catholicism by coming to an agreement with Charles I. It was an impossible task, doomed not only by Charles's reluctance to enter such an agreement but also by Rinuccini's brand of militant Catholicism, which regarded any form of compromise as treachery.

In England, the parliamentary forces quickly became openly hostile to the Confederation, but the king played a cat-and-mouse game. On the one hand, he needed confederate money and arms, on the other, he could not grant their demands because he would lose support in England by accommodating perceived rebels. The king's principal negotiator was James Butler (1610–1688), the twelfth earl of Ormonde, who successfully arranged a one-year truce with the confederates. During this truce, the final terms of agreement were to be worked out between the confederates and the king. However, Ormonde, who was kept informed by his supporters and tenants of almost every move in Kilkenny, showed no desire to reach an early settlement, and instead of being resolved in one year the talks dragged on over five years. The swirl of unresolved negotiations, sometimes secret, sometimes not, sometimes in Ireland, at others in England, generated dissension and distrust among the confederates and accentuated the existing divisions between Old English, Gaelic Irish, moderates and local supporters of Ormonde. These difficulties were compounded by the lack of a unified military command and by the blinkered leadership of religious zealots. In particular, the papal nuncio, Rinuccini, in whom so much hope was placed, proved to be politically intransigent. By the time the confederates decided to ignore him and to appeal directly to Rome, whatever chance they might have had of achieving their aims was lost. In fairness, no one in Kilkenny could have foreseen, even as late as 1647, that parliament would put the king on trial for his life, and no one could have prophesied a forthcoming commonwealth or republic. With the execution of Charles I, however, all confederate hope ended. A little over six months later, on August 15 1649, a parliamentary army under the control of Oliver Cromwell landed at Dublin and in March 1650, after a siege lasting one week, Kilkenny surrendered.

Cromwellian Kilkenny, 1650–1659

Saying that he had come 'not to destroy but to cherish them', Cromwell levied a fine on Kilkenny's inhabitants of £2000 sterling (which was, incidentally, sixty-six times the value of Rothe House, perhaps £66 million in today's terms) and appointed Colonel Daniel Axtell as their military governor. At first, Kilkenny was permitted to retain its mayor, corporation and privileges, but shortly afterwards they were suppressed and instructions were issued that the property of all citizens was to be confiscated. Under Axtell's patronage, a Baptist community developed in the town. Although Catholic clergy were required to leave, some priests continued to minister. In 1653, however, a Decree of Banishment was published against all Catholic clergy. Those who did not comply were arrested and one priest, who defied the Decree, was executed.

In 1654 the Order of Confiscation was issued by the government of Ireland. Kilkenny was to be cleared and its citizens transplanted to Connacht. The order proved extremely difficult to implement, however, because the economic infrastructure that kept the city functioning consisted of the bonds and links built up between the Catholic (Old English) families. In practice, it was simpler to lease some of the confiscated houses to their original occupants rather than to risk the total breakdown of supply routes and the consequent starvation of all the inhabitants that it might bring. Some householders, however, were exiled to Connacht. Subsequently, they complained that they were forced to move at the worst time of the year and that their goods received only a fraction of their value at auction because of the glut on the market. It was only the wealthier sector of society that had to move; servants and manual labourers were required to stay and serve their new masters.

At the time of this transplantation, or immediately afterwards, the city was surveyed and valued with a view to reallocating its properties. The resulting document, the *Civil Survey*, provides an insight into the building fabric and appearance of the city in 1654. It is incomplete, but the surviving fragment lists over 200 residential buildings, sixty-three percent of which were stone-built with roofs of slate, sixteen percent had stone walls and thatched roofs, while twenty-one percent were constructed of wattles and clay and were also thatched. The stone houses, and also the largest houses, were concentrated in Castle Street (now the Parade) and High Street (including the later Parliament Street). Patrick Street had surprisingly few stone houses, but this may reflect the incomplete nature of the record rather than the reality on the ground. The majority of the wattle-and-clay houses, the dwellings of the town's poor, were located on the lanes and side streets off High Street. Gardens were evenly spread across the town, but there was a noticeable concentration of orchards between Parliament Street/St Kieran Street and the River Nore.

In 1656 the corporation was restored and Abel Warren was appointed mayor. One of its first acts was to grant three Catholics the right to vote – Walter Archer, James Bryan and Edward Rothe – a clear indication that members of the old merchant community managed to survive Cromwell's clearances. In an example of puritan zeal, however, instructions were also issued to arrest anyone found drinking or playing cards during the times of divine service. There are indications that much of the city's trade had already collapsed. The corporation described the city as being in decay, and when repairs were ordered for St Canice's Cathedral and St Mary's Church, the corporation appealed for contributions from the citizens because its former sources of revenue no longer existed. In the census of c.1659, the population of the city was put at 1,311, about one quarter of whom (359 people) were New English. The real totals, however, when children and the very poor are included, were probably double these numbers. The majority of the New English (220 people) lived within the walls of Hightown, where they constituted just over half of the population. Within Hightown, the settlers were concentrated in High Street and Castle Street, where they formed seventy-three percent of the population. The larger, wealthier and more secure of the older stone-built properties within the walls were the ones occupied by the new Cromwellian settlers.

Funerary monument in St Mary's churchyard.

The Restoration, 1660–1687

Oliver Cromwell died in 1658 and the commonwealth he had created existed for less than two more years before Charles II was restored to the English throne in 1660. Kilkenny's fortunes improved with the Restoration because James Butler, who had gone into exile in France with Charles II, was restored to favour, created duke of Ormonde at the coronation in 1661 and once more appointed as lord lieutenant of Ireland. Ormonde's proximity to the centres of power meant that he was able to regain some of the confiscated properties (particularly Butler ones). He made his dislike for the Cromwellian corporation clear by claiming the entire city as his on the grounds that, at the outbreak of the rebellion in 1641, he had been granted all forfeited property within his territories. He obtained a charter to this effect from Charles II, listing over 185 properties in the town, but the corporation fought him tooth-and-nail and spun the proceedings out for fifteen years. In 1676 a settlement was concluded whereby Ormonde received rents worth about one-tenth of what he had claimed.

Effectively, only lands held by regicides (those who had participated directly in the execution of Charles I) were confiscated by the Restoration regime. This was good news for some in Kilkenny, because Colonel Daniel Axtell had been the officer in charge of the guard at the execution of Charles I. Accordingly, a few of the Old English families managed to regain their houses, but large numbers of hopefuls remained unsatisfied.

After his return, Ormonde transformed the castle and had a substantial impact on the appearance of the town. With the exception of the hall and gallery, built in the 1560s, Kilkenny Castle had largely remained a medieval fortress, but the duke set about converting it into a French-style château. English and French gardeners were employed to redesign the gardens, a French fontainier constructed a fountain with a jet of twenty-four feet and an elaborate water-house, with a summer banqueting room, was built. The duke had the east side of Castle Street demolished in order to create the Parade, a new formal approach to the castle that integrated it directly with the town for the first time. He established a new grammar school, Kilkenny College, in 1684; he upgraded the inns; and, in 1676, he enhanced the corporation's civic regalia by presenting them with the great silver mace that is still used on all public occasions.

The Frenchified, chateâu-like appearance of Kilkenny Castle about 1800, before it was given its present baronial façade.

The Restoration also brought Catholic priests back to the town. There were twelve in 1660 and fourteen in 1662, while a Franciscan priest had already returned in 1658. By 1667 there were four parish chapels, as well as a Jesuit chapel, a Capuchin friary, a Dominican house and a Franciscan house. There were also five schools, one of which was run by the Jesuits. Ormonde was clearly worried about the high visibility of Catholicism and he communicated to the mayor his wish that Mass should not be celebrated within the walls of the town. By 1678 all four parish chapels were located immediately outside the walls.

Control of the corporation had remained in the hands of Cromwellians since 1660. Catholics were excluded from office by the Oath of Supremacy, which required all public officials to renounce the rights of any foreign jurisdictions (ie, Rome) to make appointments in Ireland and to accept the English king as the supreme ruler of the Church. With the accession of James II in 1685, however, and the abandonment of the Oath of Supremacy, Catholics began to play a more prominent role in civic life. A new Catholic college was opened in 1686. In 1687 the city was granted a new governing charter, and a new mayor and aldermen, belonging to the Catholic Old English families, were appointed. The new corporation made a gesture towards inclusiveness and admitted a handful of Cromwellians, among them Josias Haydocke, the city apothecary, who had masterminded the corporation's stance against the duke of Ormonde a decade before.

The Jacobite and Williamite town, 1689–1691

James II's pro-Catholic and pro-French policies provoked a revolt in England. The English throne was offered to his son-in-law, the staunchly anti-French Prince William of Orange. A *coup d'état* was arranged in England; James II was ousted and forced to flee to France. In March 1689, James landed at Kinsale, County Cork, and proceeded, via Kilkenny, to Dublin, where the Irish parliament declared the lands of Protestant supporters of William of Orange, such as the second duke of Ormonde, to be forfeit.

James II appears to have disliked Dublin and instead spent most of the winter months, from November 1689 until January 1690, at Kilkenny, residing at the castle. During this time he elevated the Catholic college, which had taken over the premises of Kilkenny College, into a university: the Royal College of St Canice. Six months later, after James's defeat by William of Orange at the Battle of the Boyne, the university was forced to close. James's retreating army passed through Kilkenny on its way to Limerick and forced the townspeople to pay protection money in order to prevent them from looting the city. Kilkenny surrendered to the Williamites without firing a shot, and the propertied Old English families, who had supported James almost to a man, lost everything. Several decamped and followed the army to Limerick and eventually went into exile on the Continent, where they served in the armies of France, Spain, Austria and Russia.

The second duke of Ormonde, who had fought with William at the Boyne, raced ahead so that he would be present to receive the king in state at the castle. The Williamite army, commanded by General Godert de Ginkel, camped beside Kilkenny, making the town its winter headquarters from October 1690 until May 1691, when it moved on to besiege Limerick. Before entering Kilkenny, William III suspended the corporation and replaced it with an exclusively Protestant body. There was a clean sweep of the old regime.

It is interesting to note, in passing, that of the old council members, only Josias Haydocke, described in 1684 as 'a cunning man ... [who] will play his part better behind the curtain than upon the open stage', displayed that greatest of political skills – survival – and was appointed to the new council. He died three years later, shortly after he had been elected MP for the city. His career personified the tenacity, endurance and will to succeed of the new Kilkenny elite.

View of Green's Bridge and Irishtown, about 1800.

The eighteenth- and nineteenth-century city

The mayor graphically expressed the continuing tension between the new Protestant elite and the Catholic middle class when he complained in 1708 that:

> **The Protestants of this city are but a handful faced with an inveterate and implacable enemy.**

Protestants who married Catholics were excluded from civic office, but this proved unenforceable because the marriage pool was so small and it was waived in 1697. The application of the Penal Laws led to the closure of all Catholic churches in 1698, but within a few years the restrictions were eased and the churches began to function again. The construction, also in 1698, of infantry barracks in the old St John's Priory, and of cavalry barracks in the former Franciscan friary, increased the elite's sense of security. Despite the localised terror occasionally generated by agrarian protesters, such as the Whiteboys, and the rebellion of 1798, the strength of the garrison ensured that Kilkenny was largely untouched by revolution or military violence until the 1920s.

In the census of 1702 there were 292 Protestant families and 715 Catholic families in the city, making a total of 1,007 families and a population of perhaps 5,000. Despite the increase in population since 1659, the corporation pointed out in 1704 that there were many vacant houses in the city. In 1731, Protestant families formed less than twenty percent of the total number of inhabitants and the Protestant population probably reached a peak in the 1730s or 1740s, declining gradually thereafter. By 1800 the Protestant population constituted five percent of the total. The decline of the Protestant percentage of the population has been attributed primarily to the fact that Kilkenny's growth in population throughout the eighteenth century was due to migration from the city's rural Catholic hinterland, whereas immigration from England was negligible.

In 1691 the house of Ormonde had never enjoyed greater power or prestige, but within twenty-five years it had dropped to an all-time low. In 1715 the second duke was scapegoated and impeached for the British Army's failure in Flanders during the War of the Spanish Succession. His estates were forfeited and he went into exile in France, where he remained a prominent Jacobite supporter until his death in 1745. The absence of a great lord meant that no one dominated the

The Tholsel.

eighteenth-century town in the manner in which the first duke and his medieval predecessors had controlled it. While the corporation increased its autonomy from the castle, urban politics in the eighteenth century revolved around minor personalities whose sole pursuit was family control of patronage, rather than social issues or philosophies. The exclusion of Catholics meant that the pool of political talent, always small, was further reduced and power had to move from the business class, still essentially Catholic, to the only other group that could provide leadership: the country gentry.

Throughout the eighteenth century, and for part of the nineteenth, urban politics was dominated by families, mostly of Cromwellian origin, who lived outside the city: the Agars, Blunts, Blundens, Cuffes, Helshams, Langrishes, Morres, Wandesfords and Wemys. Between them they operated an oligarchic control of the town every bit as total as that of their Shee, Archer and Rothe precursors, but with the important difference that the new governing elite resided in country houses, miles outside the town.

Architecturally, the rule of the gentry is reflected not in the construction of private mansions but in the remodelling and enlargement of public buildings such as the Tholsel, the Courthouse, the two bridges (rebuilt after a great flood in 1763) and semi-public structures such as Kilkenny College. The enlarged Tholsel was a rebuilding of the sixteenth-century structure that strove to retain the character of the original, while the remodelled courthouse was essentially a classical building erected on top of its sixteenth-century predecessor. The message was that, although power might have shifted, it was business as usual. A number of Georgian town houses were built, but the grand private dwellings of this period were the Deanery and the remodelled Bishop's Palace, an indication that the only town residents belonging to the ruling class were churchmen.

The textile industry

Economic development in Kilkenny during the seventeenth and eighteenth centuries was characterised by the increasing exploitation of natural resources, but the foundation of the city's prosperity remained its rich agricultural hinterland and, in particular, the sale of cattle and grain. The industrial use of the rivers Nore and Bregagh intensified with the construction of several new mills, the introduction of new treatments for textiles and the development of a brewing industry.

Frieze – a rough, heavy, woollen cloth – was manufactured during the second half of the seventeenth century, but competition from Carrick-on-Suir forced the Kilkenny weavers to produce worsted, a finer quality fabric. Although subject to fluctuating demand, the woollen industry, and blanket manufacturing in particular, was the city's principal source of employment throughout the eighteenth century. Most of the wool sold at the Kilkenny markets went to Cork or Carrick-on-Suir, while the wool used to manufacture the upmarket Kilkenny blankets was a lambswool brought from Dublin. Around the middle of the century, the Ormonde Mills, which had functioned for almost six hundred years as grain mills, were converted to woollen mills, and the Maudlin Mills also became woollen mills before 1792. A review of the industry in 1800 (published in 1802) states that there were fifty working looms providing employment to about 780 people, or five percent of the entire population. By 1821 eleven woollen manufacturers directly employed 765 people, who were said to have nearly 2,500 dependants.

By 1841, however, the Ormonde Woollen Mills could no longer afford to employ its weavers. The industry declined largely because of the failure to industrialise, but also because the free trade philosophy of the time required the lifting of protective tariffs and the Irish market was quickly flooded with cheap English blankets. The Ormonde Woollen Mills was revived in the 1860s and struggled on until its destruction by fire in 1969.

Several attempts were made to introduce the linen industry. In 1701 a Huguenot, William Crommellin, brother of Louis Crommellin who established a linen manufactory at Lisburn in County Antrim in 1698, was settled in the city by the second duke of Ormonde. His business proved unsuccessful and appears to have ceased by 1709.

Shortly before 1763, the Lintown Weaving School at Green's Hill was founded by the Church of Ireland bishop and noted traveller Richard Pococke (1704–1765). This was a school in which previously uneducated Catholic boys, between the ages of twelve and sixteen, were taught linen-weaving together with reading and writing, and 'were instructed in the principles of the Protestant religion'. The school had a factory attached to it and its products were highly regarded. By 1825, however, its educational function had ceased, on investigation the 'boys' were found to be adults and the school had become a money-making venture for the master. It ceased producing linen in 1839.

Bleach greens, for bleaching cloth, were established on both sides of the Nore, at a short distance from the city, in the 1780s and 1790s, and there are surviving illustrations of flax set out to dry in the grounds of Kilkenny College. Despite these endeavours the linen industry remained unsuccessful, essentially because there was no incentive to grow flax in an area where corn flourished.

'Marble' and coal

Throughout the Middle Ages, the Black Quarry functioned as the common quarry of the town, from which both burgesses and freemen drew building stone freely. By the eighteenth century, however, the quarry was in private hands – the transition from public to private use probably occurred as part of the land changes in the Cromwellian and Restoration periods. The quarry provided the best quality limestone in the vicinity of the town, and when the stone was polished it had a distinctive dark-black colour. This polished limestone, or 'marble' as it was called, became the basis of an important eighteenth- and nineteenth-century industry and gave Kilkenny its nickname of 'the marble city'.

By the 1730s the greater part of the Black Quarry was worked by William Colles, who established the Kilkenny Marble Works on the east bank of the River Nore at Maddoxtown, about 5km south of the city. Some coarse work was carried out at the quarry; the blocks were brought to a marble yard in the city, where some were split and polished. A substantial inland trade developed and fireplaces, cisterns, bowls, vases and mirror frames were the principal finished products. The Napoleonic Wars (1800–1815) provided a boost to the market because of the blockade on Italian marble, but after 1815 the industry seems to have gradually declined. It was revived again in the 1850s and survived, on a small scale, into the 1920s.

Throughout the eighteenth century, Kilkenny was synonymous with coal, although the mines were located 20km north of the city. The first pits were sunk near Castlecomer shortly after 1700, the coal was marketed at Kilkenny and shipped southwards through it. The collieries enriched their owners – the Wandesford family – and towards the close of the eighteenth century, it was marriage to the Wandesford heiress (*see* Butler family tree, p.29) that restored the Ormonde fortunes. The trade in coal was substantial and was such a high-profile activity by the middle of the eighteenth century that the northern end of High Street was named Coal Market (now Parliament Street).

Brewing

One of the major industrial changes of the post-medieval period was the shift from private brewing, a traditional right of the town's freemen, to commercial brewing. It was obviously in the interests of the commercial brewers to restrict private brewing, and throughout the eighteenth century rewards were offered for information leading to the closure of private breweries.

Sullivan's Brewery, formerly James's St Brewery, the oldest brewery in Kilkenny, photographed about 1950.

The first brewery that can be linked directly with a family is Archdeakin's Brewery (later James's Street Brewery), established in 1702 in what was almost certainly a pre-existing brewing premises. Smithwicks, the best-known Kilkenny brewers, acquired Brennan's Distillery in 1827 and established St Francis's Abbey Brewery. Despite the impression that there was a mass market for alcoholic beverages in the eighteenth and nineteenth centuries, the brewing business itself was a very uncertain one. In 1787, for instance, there were ten breweries in the town, by 1824 the number had declined to five, and in 1837 it had fallen to four. By 1856 there were only two functioning firms: St Francis's Abbey (Smithwicks) and James's Street (Sullivans).

The collapse of the local brewing industry around the middle of the nineteenth century resulted from the coming together of a number of factors. Firstly, local ale tended to be of poor quality because it was brewed for immediate consumption, so consumers switched to porter once it became available. Secondly, the brewers' traditional local-scale economy meant they could not compete with larger outside concerns. Thirdly, the population decline from the 1830s onwards, coupled with the rise of Father Matthew's Temperance Movement (advocating total abstinence from alcohol), which had started in Kilkenny in 1838, meant that there were far fewer customers than before. Smithwicks and Sullivans managed to survive by expanding their markets to England and Wales. The development of the British tied-house system, however, which linked individual public houses with specific brewers, forced Irish breweries out of the British market and James's Street Brewery had closed by the beginning of the First World War. Smithwicks, who, in the course of the twentieth century, established themselves as one of the leading Irish brand names, subsequently acquired its premises.

Transport

The city lay on the main road between Dublin and Cork, and road improvements turned it into a busy centre for coach transport. The first horse-drawn coach service to Dublin appears to have commenced about 1730. By the 1770s there was a daily service to Dublin, giving the city a more regular postal service than that of many other inland towns.

The failure to build a canal, despite many efforts, which would have made the city navigable from the sea, was to have an enduring impact. It led to the development of rival market places, notably Bagenalstown (County Carlow) on the River Barrow and Clonmel (County Tipperary) on the River Suir, from where it was cheaper to ship goods to Dublin and Waterford.

By the late 1840s, when the railways arrived, most of Kilkenny's manufacturing industries were in decline. The lifeline that the railways might have provided was weakened by the fact that the city was on the boundary of territory controlled by two rival companies. A parliamentary act of 1845 enabled the Waterford and Kilkenny Railway (W&KR) to construct a line between the two cities, and, by 1848, eleven miles had been laid, linking Kilkenny with Thomastown. It was not until 1864, however, that the connection with Waterford was achieved. The Great Southern and Western Railway (GS&WR) built the line between Dublin and Carlow in 1846, and extended it to Kilkenny in 1850. But for the last two miles of the journey, from Kilkenny (Lavistown) Junction, the GS&WR trains had to travel over W&KR track, and this proved to be such a source of contention that in 1867 the GS&WR laid a second line. This did not solve the problem, however. Bitter disagreement between the companies meant that cattle and other goods frequently had to be off-loaded from one wagon and placed on another, and the GS&WR scheduled its services so that it was quicker to get to Dublin from Waterford via Limerick rather than via Kilkenny. This awkward situation improved when the GS&WR eventually absorbed its rival in 1900, but not before the rivalry had had an adverse effect on Kilkenny businesses.

Education

Between 1790 and 1840 small private schools and academies flourished in the city and offered, to those who could afford it, a training in English, French, classics, mathematics and music. The private schools gradually increased in number until the mid-1830s, when they declined as a result of government reform and investment in public education. During the first quarter of the nineteenth century, however, private schools evidently provided substantial revenue for the city. Several Catholic schools existed in the early eighteenth-century city, but it was not until the Penal Laws were relaxed that such schools became a prominent feature.

Burrell's Hall, on the site now occupied by St Mary's Cathedral,

St Kieran's College.

opened as the diocesan ecclesiastical college in 1783; a year later, two free schools, catering for poorer Catholics, were set up in Chapel Lane. In 1800 the Presentation Convent School was established, initially for twelve girls, but by 1818 it had expanded to 300 girls. This group of schools was located in the same area (as were the later Christian Brothers' schools at Tilbury Place and James's Street) forming a sector of Catholic education around St Mary's Cathedral and the Bishop's Palace. Architecturally, the schools were unpretentious, but with the passing of the Catholic Emancipation Act in 1829 (permitting Catholics to hold government positions and to sit in parliament), their profile was heightened and they developed into sizeable building complexes. Taken together with the construction of the new St Mary's Cathedral between 1843 and 1857, the largest and most prominent building in the city, these developments proclaimed the arrival of the Catholic middle class as a powerful force in city life. A similar confidence is displayed in the neo-Tudor design of St Kieran's College, the new diocesan college, which was built in 1836 within extensive parkland on the southwestern side of the city.

Leisure interests

The eighteenth and nineteenth centuries saw the development of important service industries such as banking, insurance and printing. Booksellers and circulating libraries first appeared in the eighteenth century, but little is known either of their duration or success. Other leisure interests that developed in the eighteenth century included bowling and tennis, while the foundation of the Club House in 1797, established initially as a fox-hunting club, provided a social forum in which men could meet.

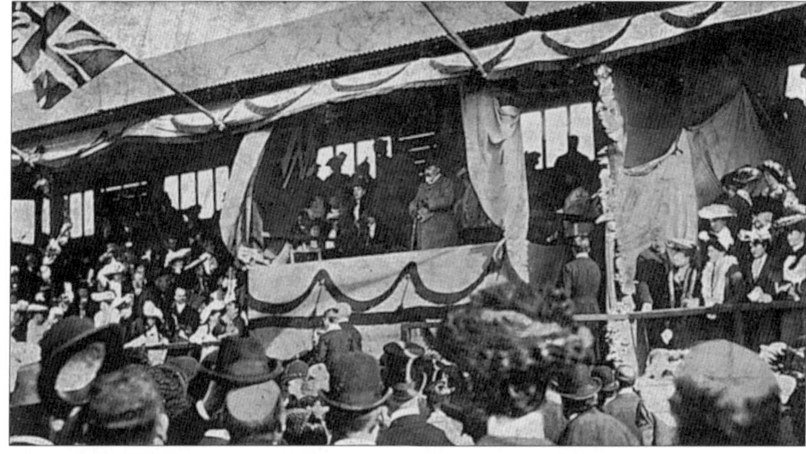

King Edward VII at the Kilkenny Agricultural Show, 1904.

From the 1780s until the 1820s, however, the principal social event was the annual theatre season, which lasted for a month. The performances were produced initially by visiting companies, but the foundation of the Kilkenny Players initiated a phase of gentleman actors. Visiting companies performed in the Tholsel or in the Courthouse, but the gentleman players constructed their own theatre on the Parade in 1805. For the next fourteen years the Kilkenny season was one of the highlights of the Irish social calendar, with fox-hunting and races during the day, evening balls and concerts held at the Tholsel, the castle and the theatre itself, and private balls at the Club House. The lord lieutenant and his entourage were regular visitors, and it was said that mothers with marriageable daughters found Kilkenny next best to Bath, in England, for finding eligible husbands. The plays were performed for charity. A box seat cost six shillings, which was one and a half times a labourer's weekly wage, or the equivalent of hiring a carpenter, mason or blacksmith for three days. The productions usually raised about £200 per annum, but in one season £1,000 was donated to Kilkenny charities.

A more enduring cultural group is the Kilkenny Archaeological Society. It became a national organisation within a decade of its foundation in 1849, due to its vigorous campaign for the preservation of Ireland's ancient monuments. In 1890 it was designated the Royal Society of Antiquaries of Ireland and, within a few years, moved its headquarters to Dublin, where its museum was incorporated within the National Museum of Ireland on Kildare Street.

Population decline and famine

By the middle of the nineteenth century, almost two-thirds of the city's population consisted of poor people, who lived in mud cabins. Most of these cabins consisted of a single, dark, smoke-filled room, with neither a chimney nor a window. Internal furnishings were basic, consisting of straw beds and stools, when they could be afforded, and a peat fire for cooking. The poor person's diet consisted of potatoes, butter and milk, which were eaten for breakfast, dinner and supper. Occasionally a herring or an egg might be available, but meat was almost unknown. The poor were essentially dependent on the potato, and if anything should happen to the potato crop their lives could be at risk.

In the course of the eighteenth and nineteenth centuries, central government gradually replaced the landlords and gentry as the source of authority. There followed the establishment, usually on the city's periphery, of public institutions such as infirmaries, fever hospitals, workhouses and a jail. The buildings themselves were deliberately built to appear gloomy and depressing. It is unsurprising, if regrettable, that very few fragments of these buildings survive. Conditions in these institutions, however, provide an insight into the life of the urban underclass.

The Kilkenny Workhouse, which was opened by 1841, was ostensibly established for the relief of the poor and destitute, but relief was given only in return for work, hence the name 'workhouse'. The workhouse was maintained at public expense and to keep costs at a minimum people were discouraged from entering it. The food, clothing and lodging provided in the workhouse were poorer than those available to working labourers in the town.

Few people died of starvation in Kilkenny during the Great Famine (1845–1849), but thousands died of disease caused by the Famine.

In order to qualify for relief, the entire family had to enter the workhouse. The family was separated on admission, men and women were segregated and children over two years of age were sent to separate children's wards. An adult received two meals a day. Breakfast comprised eight ounces of porridge and a half-pint of milk, while dinner consisted of three and a half pounds of potatoes and one pint of skimmed milk. The inmates rose at 7am and went to bed at 8pm. Idleness was not permitted, although the inmates had to work without receiving payment. The men broke stones, ground corn and worked on the land attached to the workhouse. The women washed and mended clothes and looked after the children. Smoking, drinking and card-playing were prohibited. Nothing short of destitution would compel anyone to seek refuge in a workhouse. In the course of the Great Famine (1845–1849), however, the Kilkenny Workhouse, built to accommodate 1,300 paupers, was home to over 4,000 people.

Potato blight was first reported in Ireland in August 1845 and by October it had reached Kilkenny. About two-thirds of the potato crop was saved, but in the following year, 1846, the potato crop was almost totally destroyed by the blight. The shortfall pushed up the price of potatoes and, for the very poor, the workhouse became their only option for survival. In February 1847 soup kitchens were set up at several points within the city to feed the needy – almost 1,000 people were served on a daily basis. Hundreds of starving people flocked into the city in order to obtain relief. On 27 March, the *Kilkenny Journal* stated that 'never was there such a large amount of paupers in Kilkenny – the streets are swarming with beggars, and fever and dysentery are widespread'. In their desire to alleviate the sufferings of the poor, the workhouse governors ran up an enormous debt and, quite illegally, fed people who were not entitled to be admitted to the workhouse. Due to the prompt action of the workhouse governors, very few people died of starvation in the city. There was a deadlier killer, however. The overcrowded conditions provided an ideal place for the spread of infection and disease. Between 1846 and 1848 over 2,000 workhouse inmates, as well as the master of the workhouse, died of relapsing fever, which was transmitted by ticks and lice. Mortality was highest among the poor, but typhus, which was also transmitted by lice, carried away many members of the higher social classes.

The population of most Irish cities gradually recovered from the devastation of the Great Famine, but Kilkenny's did not. In truth, however, the population decline was already well under way by the time the famine struck. In 1831 the city had a population of 23,741, but a year later there was a severe cholera epidemic that killed 1,500 people. From that time onwards the numbers continued to decline. By 1841 the population had dropped to 19,000; in 1861 it was just 14,000; by 1901 it had fallen to 10,000. The Great Famine merely accelerated an existing trend. The continuing decline in population owed more to the city's failure to industrialise than it did to the starvation and dislocation of the Famine years.

With the aid of hindsight, the decline of nineteenth-century Kilkenny may be traced to two factors. Firstly, the conviction for treason of the second duke of Ormonde in 1715, which led to the removal of the town's most active improver. Secondly, the failure to build a canal in the 1750s and 1760s led to a loss of trade, which meant that there was little local capital with which to industrialise in the early 1800s. The city's woollen mills and blanket manufactories functioned only for as long as they could pay exploitatively cheap wages. Once tariffs were raised and mass-produced English goods flooded the market in the 1830s, the woollen industry was unable to adapt. It was, perhaps, the psychological trauma of the Famine and the absence of any economic revival in its aftermath that directed minds towards emigration, and for the next one hundred and fifty years the city continued to lose more people than it gained. Only in the 1950s did the population climb to 12,000. By the 1970s it had returned to late eighteenth-century levels, but even today the population still remains short of early nineteenth-century figures.

Kilkenny in the twentieth century

It has been observed that Kilkenny slept through most of the twentieth century. Except for a week-long siege of Kilkenny Castle, the city was largely unaffected by the War of Independence (1919–1921) or by the subsequent Civil War (1922–1923).

The Tholsel was the venue for the proclamation of George V as king, 1910.

The castle itself gradually fell into decay as declining rents and the new political climate after independence made the city unattractive as a residence for the Butler family. In 1935 the contents of the castle were auctioned and the family moved from Ireland.

Well into the second half of the twentieth century, the principal industries remained exactly the same as those of the 1830s – brewing, shoemaking, woollen manufacturing and ironworking (gradually replaced by 'light engineering') – but almost all were practised on a smaller scale than in the 1830s. There were positive developments, however, in the form of improved medical facilities, better access roads, local authority housing and the provision of leisure resources such as cinemas and playing fields. Hurling was a significant part of sporting and social life throughout the century. The black and amber shirts of the county team have been worn by many outstanding players from the city, and the team has won the coveted All-Ireland Final on twenty-five occasions – a record surpassed only by County Cork.

The foundation of the Kilkenny Design Workshops in 1965 (a government-sponsored body charged with promoting good design in Irish industry), attracted a colony of artists and craftspeople who have played an active role in developing the city's cultural life. They were largely responsible for launching the annual Kilkenny Arts Week in 1974, which, with its concerts, exhibitions and readings, is one of the major features of the cultural year. The Cat Laughs Festival, which is devoted to stand-up comedy, was established in 1995 and has acquired an international reputation. The Kilkenny Chess Club, founded in 1970, has proved to be very successful. Its annual Masters' Tournament is one of the few sporting events in Ireland that regularly attracts contestants of world championship class.

The *Corpus Christi* procession, High Street, 1947.

The new Kilkenny Archaeological Society (not to be confused with the first society, now the Royal Society of Antiquaries of Ireland), founded in 1945, proved to be a progressive, far-sighted force. The society's purchase and reconstruction of Rothe House in 1966 highlighted the importance of the city's architectural heritage, and the members campaigned with steady success for the conservation of the urban fabric. The restoration of Rothe House gave the people of Kilkenny a new-found pride in their past. Further restorations followed – at Kyteler's Inn, the Shee Almshouse and Kilkenny Castle. The society's work prepared the way for the tourism industry of the 1980s and 1990s. The restored Kilkenny Castle, presented, together with its parkland, to the citizens of Kilkenny in 1967 by Arthur Butler, sixth marquess of Ormonde, is now one of the major tourist attractions in the southeast.

Kilkenny is one of the most visually enchanting Irish cities, and it was, in fact, an advantage for today's inhabitants that the city 'slept' through most of the twentieth century. The absence of wealth meant that, until the 1990s, urban renewal was very limited. Shopowners

High Street, showing the Tholsel undergoing repairs, about 1953.

simply could not afford to demolish old buildings and replace them with new ones. In the 1980s by-laws were introduced to protect the city's traditional shop-fronts and interiors, many of which were built between 1890 and 1910. With the changing economic circumstances of the 1990s, however, and the influx of new money as part of the 'Celtic tiger' economy, a spate of building was initiated. Much of this new construction work lacked sensitivity to the city's historic environment and resulted in several unfortunate developments. The construction of large hotel complexes, shopping malls, high-rise car parks and apartment blocks, designed to service both the expanding population and the increasing numbers of visitors, has resulted in the obliteration of much of the city's historic fabric and environment. Conservationists have observed that more damage occurred to the building fabric of Kilkenny in the decade between 1990 and 2000 than was ever achieved by the artillery of Oliver Cromwell. Only time will tell whether the short-term improvement in services will outweigh the long-term reduction of the city's environmental quality.

The most far-reaching development of the last fifty years, however, may be completely unrelated to any of the above. The expansion of Smithwick's Brewery, and its take-over by the Guinness Group, led, in the 1990s, to the creation of an export market and the development of a new beer: Kilkenny Ale. It is found in bars across Europe and America and, as a result of its success, Kilkenny has become a household name to virtually every adult in north-western Europe. This can only promote further interest in the city and it is to be hoped that the increased interaction between visitors and townspeople will be of mutual benefit to both.

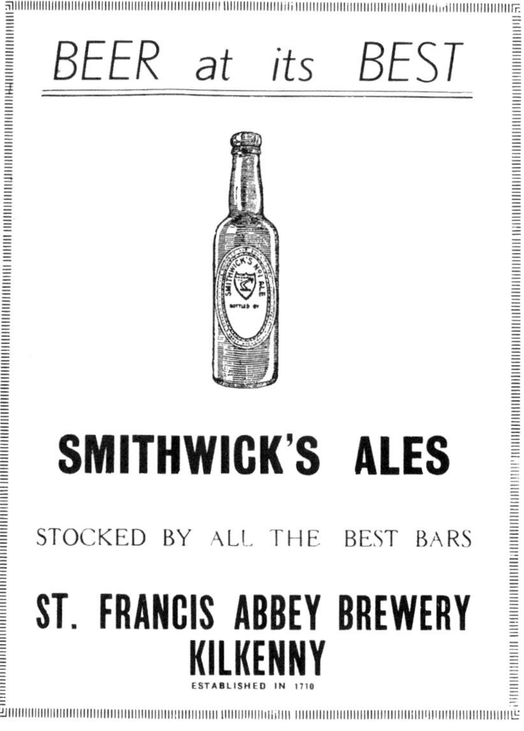

A 1947 advertisement for Smithwick's Ale.

Above: Green's Bridge, built in 1763 to a classical design based on the bridge at Rimini in Italy. (photo: Oliver of Kilkenny)

Left: 'Talbot's' Bastion, the southwestern tower of the medieval town wall, built during the thirteenth century.

Kilkenny Castle and the River Nore, viewed from near Wind Gap.

Kilkenny Castle. (photo: Oliver of Kilkenny)

The Picture Gallery, Kilkenny Castle, shortly after restoration.

Kilkenny Castle and St John's Bridge. (photo: Oliver of Kilkenny)

The medieval town wall of Kilkenny, close to the Black Abbey. (photo: Oliver of Kilkenny)

St Mary's Cathedral, built between 1843 and 1857. (photo: Oliver of Kilkenny)

St Francis's Friary. (photo: Oliver of Kilkenny)

St Canice's (Kenny's) Well, a site traditionally associated with St Canice.

St Canice's steps.
(photo: Oliver of Kilkenny)

Above: St Canice's Cathedral. (photo: Oliver of Kilkenny)

Left: Double effigy tomb of Piers Butler (d.1539), eighth earl of Ormond, and his wife, Margaret FitzGerald (d.1542) at St Canice's Cathedral.

The west doorway of St Canice's Cathedral, constructed about 1260.
(photo: Oliver of Kilkenny)

The round tower at St Canice's Cathedral.

(photo: Oliver of Kilkenny)

Above: The Dominican Friary ('Black Abbey'). The cottages on the right were demolished to create a car park on the occasion of a visit to the city by Patrick Hillery, president of Ireland. (photo: Oliver of Kilkenny)

Right: Stained glass window in the Black Abbey. The glass is of German manufacture and dates to about 1900.

Traditional Kilkenny shop-front, dating to about 1900. (photo: Oliver of Kilkenny)

Kilkenny Design Workshops, an important centre of Irish quality design, located in the former stables of Kilkenny Castle.

Above: The Courthouse, Parliament Street. (photo: Oliver of Kilkenny)

Left: Well-house in the courtyard of Rothe House. The inscription records that it was built in 1604 by John Rothe and his wife, Rose Archer.

The Tholsel arcade, High Street. (photo: Oliver of Kilkenny)

A model of seventeenth-century Kilkenny, created by the author in conjunction with the Southeast Tourism Authority, now on display in St Canice's Cathedral.

High Street, looking south towards the Tholsel. (photo: Oliver of Kilkenny)

The River Nore, looking north from St John's Bridge.

Above: The Parade, a formal space laid out by James Butler, first duke of Ormonde, for public gatherings and military assemblies.

Left: Watergate, taking its name from the medieval Water Gate, which linked Hightown (Englishtown) with Irishtown.

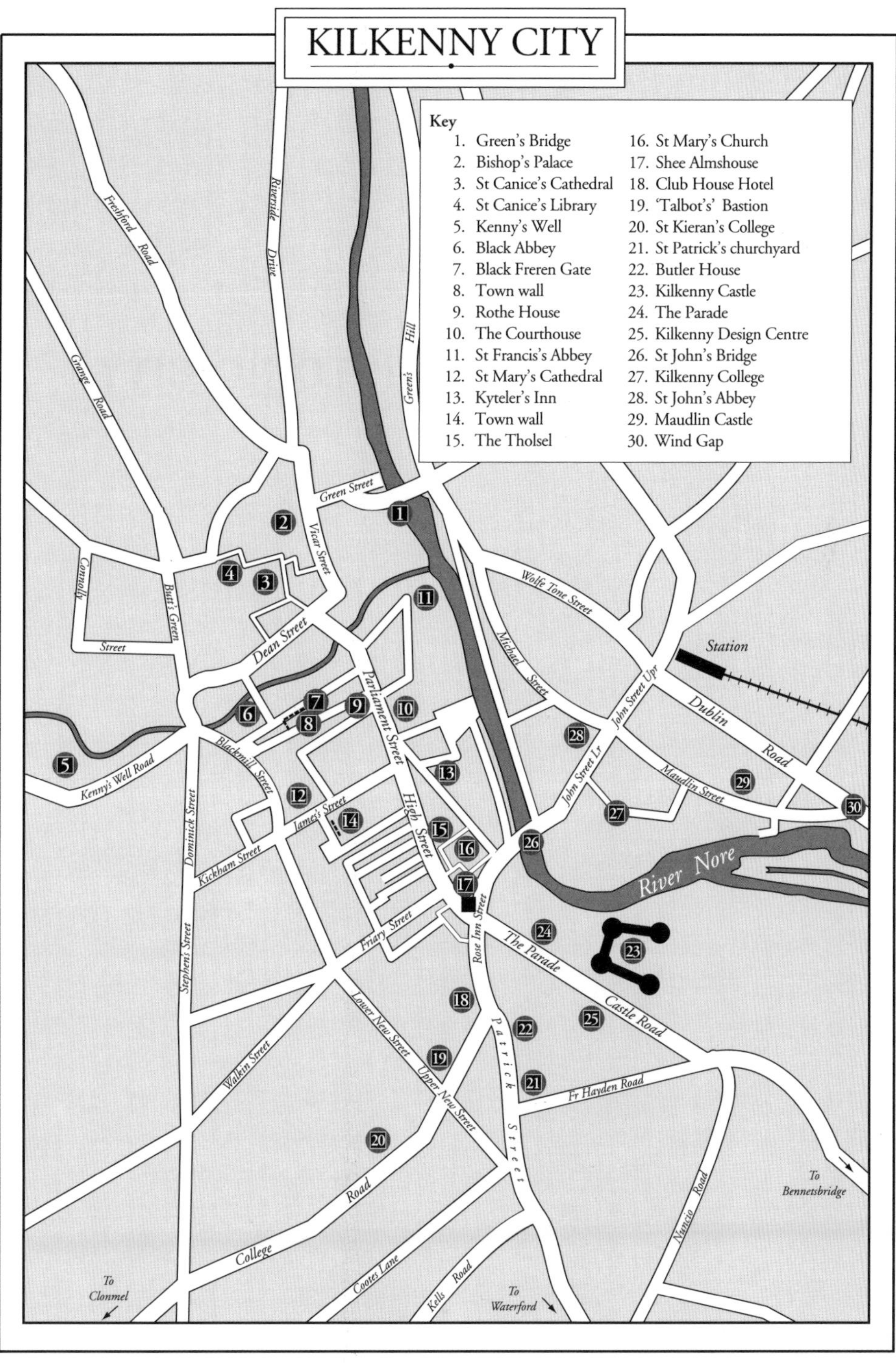

KILKENNY CITY
Key
1. Green's Bridge
2. Bishop's Palace
3. St Canice's Cathedral
4. St Canice's Library
5. Kenny's Well
6. Black Abbey
7. Black Freren Gate
8. Town wall
9. Rothe House
10. The Courthouse
11. St Francis's Abbey
12. St Mary's Cathedral
13. Kyteler's Inn
14. Town wall
15. The Tholsel
16. St Mary's Church
17. Shee Almshouse
18. Club House Hotel
19. 'Talbot's' Bastion
20. St Kieran's College
21. St Patrick's churchyard
22. Butler House
23. Kilkenny Castle
24. The Parade
25. Kilkenny Design Centre
26. St John's Bridge
27. Kilkenny College
28. St John's Abbey
29. Maudlin Castle
30. Wind Gap
Freshford Road
Riverside Drive
Green's Hill
Grange Road
Green Street
Vicar Street
Connolly Street
Butt's Green
Dean Street
Wolfe Tone Street
Michael Street
Station
Dublin Road
John Street Upr
John Street Lr
Maudlin Street
Parliament Street
Blackmill Street
Kenny's Well Road
Dominick Street
James's Street
Kickham Street
High Street
River Nore
Rose Inn Street
The Parade
Friary Street
Stephen's Street
Castle Road
Lower New Street
Upper New Street
Walkin Street
Patrick Street
Fr Hayden Road
College Road
Nuncio Road
Cootes Lane
Kells Road
To Clonmel
To Waterford
To Bennetsbridge

GUIDE TO THE HISTORIC CITY

In the course of discovering Kilkenny, it is recommended that you commence at Kilkenny Castle. Allow at least two hours to explore the castle and its former stables (now the Kilkenny Design Workshops). Allow an additional hour if you wish to walk around the castle gardens and parkland. From the castle, the recommended tour takes a zigzagging route along the axis of High Street, towards St Canice's Cathedral (allow at least two to three hours). We return from St Canice's Cathedral via the Dominican Friary and St Mary's Cathedral to High Street (allow forty minutes). We then cross to the east bank of the River Nore to explore the medieval suburb of St John's (allow forty minutes).

KILKENNY CASTLE

> ***From [Waterford] we went to Kilkenny where I saw the old castle belonging to the Ormond family kept up in the old style, and situated most beautifully on a river. There are a number of old family pictures, among which I saw my favourite Duke of Ormond's picture in King Charles I's time.***
> **(Lady Louisa Connolly of Castletown, County Kildare, 1777.)**

For many visitors, before and since Louisa Connolly, the castle and its collection of pictures form one of the highlights of a trip to Kilkenny. There is a lot to see both inside and outside the castle, and one may stroll in the parkland or relax in the gardens. Once inside the castle, visitors are taken around by guided tour and this means that, in order to make way for the next tour, your viewing time will be limited. Accordingly, I would suggest that you read (or skim) over the next few pages before going inside so that if there is something special you want to see, you will be able to make time for it. If the sun is shining, you might like to take the opportunity to sit for a few minutes in the gardens on the north side of the castle (to get your bearings, note that the formal entrance gate, with the coat of arms, is in the castle's west wing). If it is too cold, why not cross the road to the former stables, now the Kilkenny Design Centre, where, underneath the clock tower, there is a restaurant serving tea, coffee and snacks.

You can spend as much time as you like looking at the castle's exterior but, if your time is short, I have highlighted in **bold print** the features of the interior and the pictures which, for historical or artistic reasons, I think worthy of note.

The castle is intimately associated with the Butler family, who purchased it, together with a great part of County Kilkenny, in 1391. The family resided here until 1935, when the castle was closed and its contents were auctioned. In 1967, Arthur Butler, the sixth marquess of Ormonde, presented the castle and its parkland to the townspeople of Kilkenny. It was subsequently taken over by Dúchas (the Heritage Service) and is now a national monument in State care.

Arthur Butler (1893–1971), sixth marquess of Ormonde, pictured at Rothe House with members of the Kilkenny Archaeological Society, shortly after handing over Kilkenny Castle to the people of Kilkenny.

St John's Bridge and Kilkenny Castle.

As it survives today, the building reflects the nineteenth-century fashion for Baronial castles that typified the Romantic movement. This was characterised by a nostalgia for things medieval, identified with chivalry, courtliness and gentility – particularly in Britain and Ireland, where the movement was deeply influenced by the novels of Sir Walter Scott. The building was remodelled between 1825 and 1840, and its castellated Baronial appearance imitates the fashion adopted by the English royal family for their residence at Windsor Castle. In looking at the fabric of the building, it is generally easy to distinguish the original medieval stonework from the nineteenth-century additions. The medieval stonework consists of roughly quarried stones laid in somewhat irregular courses; the nineteenth-century masonry, by contrast, consists of neatly dressed and chiselled stone, fitted together with geometrical precision. The contrast is most apparent when one compares the base of the castle wall, which tends to be medieval, with the battlements and parapets at the top, which were added in the nineteenth century. The nineteenth-century stone is also slightly different in colour from the medieval work, although both came from the Black Quarry, about 1km to the south.

The first fortification on this site was an Anglo-Norman earthwork castle built before 1173. The present stone structure was commenced by William Marshall, lord of Leinster, in 1207. It was originally quadrangular in plan, with large circular drum-towers at each of the four corners, and a twin-bastioned entrance gate placed in the south wall. The south wing was badly damaged at the time of the Cromwellian siege and its remains were swept away during the nineteenth-century restorations, creating the three-sided structure that exists today.

Archaeological excavations have uncovered part of the great moat that originally enclosed the castle, and a section of it is open on the Parade wing, where a sally-port and the outlet for the medieval *garderobe* (toilet) chute can also be seen. The moat is eight metres deep and was originally defended by an outer enclosing wall. It was at least twice its present exposed width, which would have made the medieval street much narrower than its modern counterpart. The moat was filled in during the seventeenth century when the Parade was laid out as a formal approach to the castle. The exposed section of the moat provides an impression of how imposing the medieval castle would have been. Indeed, if we picture the towers without their modern windows and with only long narrow arrow slits to provide light, the fortress would have been a menacing structure.

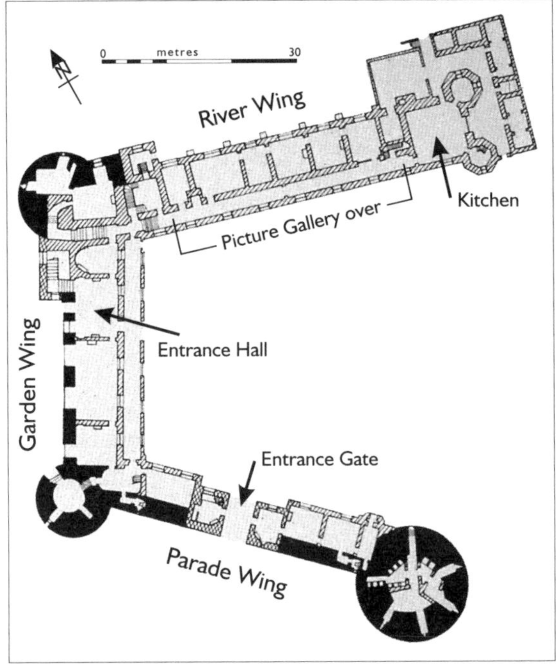

Ground plan of Kilkenny Castle (the medieval sections are shown in black).

THE ENTRANCE GATE AND THE WEST (PARADE) WING

The most striking feature on the Parade wing is the entrance gate, which is in the form of a triumphal arch. This was built shortly after 1698, when the moat had been filled in for some years and the eastern side of Castle Street had been demolished to create the Parade. It is classical in style, with a round arch, triangular pediment and Corinthian pilasters.

Below the arch is the Butler coat of arms. This consists of a quartered shield, supported on the left by a falcon and on the right by a griffin (a mythical creature with the body of a lion and the wings and head of an eagle), who is collared and chained. In the top left-hand corner of the shield is the oldest of the Butler arms: a zigzag line cutting off the upper third of the shield (known heraldically as 'chief indented') of Theobald FitzWalter (d.1205), the founder of the Butler family; in the top right-hand corner are three covered cups, symbolising the family's role as butlers to the king; in the bottom left-hand corner are the arms of the lordship of Carrick-on-Suir, another major Butler possession; while in the bottom right-hand corner is the saltire cross of the FitzGerald earls of Desmond, incorporated into the arms because the Butlers were their blood heirs. Above is the Butler motto, 'Comme je trouve', literally 'as I find', and generally understood as meaning, 'I take things as I find them'. Above the coat of arms is the Butler crest: a falcon rising from ostrich feathers inserted into a ducal coronet.

Above: The Butler coat of arms.

Left: Kilkenny Castle, entrance gate on the west (Parade) wing.

THE COURTYARD

Entrance to the castle is obtained from the courtyard, by means of a door in the north wall. If the weather is fine, you may like to sit on one of the stone benches and examine the courtyard exterior more closely. The difference between the medieval and the nineteenth-century masonry is particularly noticeable in the contrast between the southwest tower and the remainder of the building.

Aerial view of Kilkenny Castle.

To the left of the entrance door, in the Parade (west) wing, are two tall narrow windows with metal bars – these are the windows of the Muniment Room, or evidence chamber, in which the papers and charters of the Butler family were stored. Known collectively as the Ormond Deeds, they were purchased by the State about 1947 and are now housed in the National Library of Ireland, Dublin. They range in date from a land grant of 1166 to kitchen accounts of 1910, and include the only surviving original charter of Dermot MacMurrough, king of Leinster (1134–1171), as well as documents relating to the property transactions of the Butler family over seven centuries. Ireland's record in preserving documents is a poor one and the Ormond Deeds constitute the only substantial family collection to have survived from the Middle Ages into the present. Even so, it suffered damage and depredation. In the eighteenth century, the historian Thomas Carte hauled away several cartloads of documents to write his biography of the first duke of Ormonde, and those papers are now in the Bodleian Library, Oxford. More recently, in 1963, the taoiseach of the day presented a deed of 1336, recording an agreement between the earl of Ormond and the O'Kennedy, to the president of the United States of America. The document, a key record in the locality's history, had been preserved in Kilkenny for over six hundred years; it is now in the John Fitzgerald Kennedy Library at Waltham, Massachusetts.

While in the courtyard look out for the drainpipes, four of which are still topped by the funnel-shaped lead hoppers, dated 1682, which are decorated with the crest of the first duke of Ormonde.

THE CASTLE INTERIOR

The north (garden) and east (river) wings have been restored to what they would have looked like about 1860, when the castle functioned as a Victorian country house. The ground floor of the southwest corner tower on the west (Parade) wing retains its medieval character, while the upper floors have been attractively refurbished in late twentieth-century style for use as a conference centre.

The restorers reproduced the silk wallpapers, carpets and furnishings as exactly as possible. Sometimes they succeeded in tracking down the original manufacturers and, as in the case of the drawing-room carpet, occasionally discovered that the manufacturers still possessed detailed records of what had been supplied to the castle in the nineteenth century. In the 1860s the rooms would have been cluttered, in Victorian fashion, with side tables, ornaments, busts, souvenirs and the mementoes of family lives. In a modern restoration it is not possible (nor perhaps desirable) to recreate such a lived-in feel; it is the price that has to be paid for opening the building to the public rather than just to the family and its guests.

The principal feature of the **entrance hall** is a seventeenth-century Italian marble table that is original to the castle, which, according to local legend, survived the auction of 1935 only because it was too big to be moved out of the building. It was traditionally used as a waking (funeral) table. The body of the deceased was placed upon it and mourners filed past to pay their final respects. The last member of the family to be so waked was twenty-four-year-old James Anthony Butler, viscount Thurles (1916–1940), a Spitfire pilot, who was killed during the Battle of Britain. He is buried in the castle grounds.

There are full-length portraits of James Butler (1610–1688), first duke of Ormonde, and of King Charles II (1630–1685), together with a half-length portrait of Charles II's mother, Queen Henrietta Maria (1609–1669). Beside the garden door is a photograph of Arthur Butler (1893–1971), the sixth marquess of Ormonde, who presented the castle to the townspeople of Kilkenny, and a portrait of Charles Butler (1898–1997), the seventh marquess of Ormonde, painted by Aubrey Davidson Houston. Charles Butler lived in Illinois, in the USA, and worked for many years in the Art Institute of Chicago. He had no male heirs and so the title of marquess died with him. At the time of his death, Charles Butler was also the twenty-fifth earl of Ormonde and the thirty-first Chief Butler of Ireland. These titles can now be claimed, but the claimant would have to demonstrate that he is the direct descendant, in the male line, from a previous title holder. The most likely candidate for the titles is Lord Mountgarret, whose family descends from Piers Butler (c.1467–1539), eighth earl of Ormond.

Charles Butler (1899–1997), seventh marquess of Ormonde.

From the entrance hall one climbs the stairs to the dining room. Beside the stairs is a seventeenth-century tapestry, manufactured in the Gobelin workshops at Antwerp, in the Netherlands. It is one of a series that portrayed the four elements: fire, earth, air and water. In this instance it is the element air, represented by the goddess Juno. Juno's connection with the air was twofold. Firstly, according to Homer's *Iliad*, Jupiter punished Juno for disobedience by tying anvils to her feet and suspending her from the heavens. Secondly, in Virgil's *Aeneid*, it was Juno who persuaded Aeolus, the god of the winds, to unloose the winds to aid Aeneas and his comrades, who were on the sea between Sicily and Carthage. Here, Juno is shown with the peacock, a bird that was sacred to her, as well as other birds and wind instruments.

At the top of the stairs is a depiction of the Mystic Marriage of St Catherine of Siena, based on the original by the Italian Renaissance artist Correggio (c.1469–1534). Catherine of Siena (c.1347–1380) was a Christian mystic and a member of the Dominican order. She is shown in her habit and veil, kneeling, on the right of the picture. The painting represents a particular scene from Catherine's life: Catherine prayed regularly before an image of the Virgin and Child, and one day her prayerful devotion caused the infant to turn towards her and place a ring on her finger. This act symbolised her spiritual marriage to God.

The **dining room** is located in the northeast (river) tower and affords fine views over the gardens and across the river to the former Kilkenny College. The most interesting features of the room are its keyhole plan, immediately noticeable when one looks at the ceiling, and the enormous thickness of the medieval walls, visible where the windows were punched through as part of the late seventeenth-century alterations. A second tapestry from the four elements suite is hung here. This one, with the Roman god Vulcan, represents fire. Vulcan (he is the source of the word 'volcano') is shown in his forge, standing at the anvil, hammer in hand. His assistants are Cyclops, one-eyed giants, who tend the furnace. Helmets, breastplates and weapons forged by Vulcan lie about on the floor.

Above the fireplace is the finest portrait in the Ormonde collection. This is **Sir Peter Lely's portrait of the first duke of Ormonde,** painted between 1662 and 1663. The picture hangs in the same position it occupied in the nineteenth century, but it is somewhat too high and can only be appreciated with difficulty. The duke is shown standing, dressed flamboyantly in the robes of the Order of the Garter, with his right leg protruding, showing a garter tied just below the knee. In the background is the base of a column and a richly patterned hanging, indicating stability and wealth. In his left hand is the plumed hat of the Order, while in his right hand he holds a wand, symbolising his role as lord steward of the household – a position to which he was appointed after the Restoration in 1660. The swirl of the robes and the almost ridiculous haughtiness of the pose give the painting a chivalrous intensity that evokes the era of the cavaliers. It was a version of this picture (perhaps the one in the entrance hall downstairs) that prompted the praise of Lady Louisa Connolly in 1777, and has impressed many visitors before and since.

The Order of the Garter, 'the noblest order of chivalry', was instituted in 1348 by Edward III. The popular account, doubtless apocryphal, is that while he was dancing with the countess of Salisbury (with whom Edward III was said to be having an affair), her garter snapped and fell to the floor. The king bent down and picked it up, but as he did so the dancing stopped and the assembled members of the court looked on with knowing amusement. The king tied the garter onto her leg, just below the knee, and said, 'honi soit qui mal y pense' – 'shame on him who thinks evil of it'. Afterwards, he instituted an order of knighthood, modelled on the stories of King Arthur and the Knights of the Round Table, which was called the Order of the Garter. It adopted his soundbite as its motto. Membership of the Order, which still exists, is for life and is limited to twenty-four knights.

From the dining room one progresses through the ante-room to the **drawing rooms,** which have been completely restored. The ante-room is oval and functioned as a waiting room. The pictures in the drawing rooms are original to the castle and include landscapes, portraits and copies of well-known paintings, including Anthony Van Dyck's (1599–1641) study of the children of Charles II, perhaps painted by James Gandy (1619–1689). Among the pictures are the Flemish *Landscape with Waterfall*, attributed to the circle of Nicholas Berchem (1620–1683), *The Stirrup Cup*, attributed to Dirk Maes (1656–1717) and *A Jeweller and his Family* (formerly called *The Pearl Stringers*) signed by Jan de Herdt and dated 1673.

One of the bookcases is original and it served as the model to restore the others in this room. The first duke had assembled the finest library in seventeenth-century Ireland, but it was dispersed and sold after his grandson, James, second duke of Ormonde, was found guilty of treason in 1715. The Heritage Service has acquired a nine-volume set of the works of Cicero, splendidly bound in full speckled calfskin, with the first duke's arms in gilt on each cover. It is a French translation from the Latin, published in Paris in 1670 and, hopefully, it is a sign of things that may yet return to Kilkenny.

From the drawing room one ascends, usually via the **Moorish staircase** added by the architects Deane and Woodward in 1858–1862, to the bedrooms on the second floor. The well of the staircase was designed to accommodate a winter garden, and the staircase itself is decorated with snails and frogs sculpted by Charles Harrison (1835–1903), best known for his work on the Kildare Street Club in Dublin. Two of the **bedrooms**, and a toilet that was installed for the visit of Edward VII (and consequently known as 'the throne'), have been restored and, apart from the unusually vibrant Chinese wallpaper, it is the views from these rooms across the city that are memorable. The other bedrooms have not been restored and are used by the Kilkenny Art Gallery Society to display their interesting collection of nineteenth- and twentieth-century Irish paintings, including works by Mildred Anne Butler, Paul Henry and Sir John Lavery.

THE PICTURE GALLERY

The picture gallery is the most impressive room in the castle. It was commenced in the late eighteenth century, but was given its present form in the 1860s. The impressive ceiling was designed by Benjamin Woodward (1816–1861) and built in 1860–1862. It is a **hammer-beam roof** terminating, in medieval German style, in gilded dragon's heads. The decoration of strange birds, beasts and goddesses is by John Hungerford Pollen (1820–1902), and according to local tradition the languid pre-Raphaelite ladies painted on the roof struts are his daughters. The knotwork and scrollwork, although frequently described as Celtic-inspired, are standard German fare, no doubt absorbed by Pollen while he worked as an artist on Ludwig II's fairy-tale castles in Bavaria.

Pollen also designed the **double fireplace** of white Carrara marble in the centre of the room, although Charles Harrison executed the work. It is carved with elaborate entwined foliage and has seven panels depicting incidents from Butler history. From left to right these portray: (1) the purchase of the castle by the third earl of Ormond in 1391; (2) the chief butler of Ireland offering, on behalf of the Irish nobility, the first cup of wine to the newly crowned king; (3) Richard II acting as godfather to the third earl's son, named Richard in the king's honour, on the occasion of the king's visit to Kilkenny in 1395; (4) the coat of arms of the Ormonds; (5) the first duke refusing to surrender his sword on entering the Irish House of Lords in 1634; (6) the second marchioness providing food to the poor during the Great Famine of 1845–1849; and (7) the triumphal return to Dublin of the first duke as lord lieutenant of Ireland in 1662.

Photograph taken on the occasion of the visit to Kilkenny Castle of the duke of York (later King George V) in 1899. On the wall behind are two portraits of Black Tom, tenth earl of Ormond (1530–1614), and one of Queen Victoria.

The **tapestries** are products of the Gobelin workshop at Antwerp and were made about 1660. Five pieces, from a suite of six, tell the story of Decius, one of the Roman consuls for the year 340BC, and relate to an event during the war with the Latins in which Rome finally established its supremacy over the territory of Latium. The Roman historian Livy (c.64BC–c.AD17) recounts the legend of how, as the battle was going against the Romans, Decius, in a formal ceremony, dedicated both himself and the army of the enemy to the gods of the underworld (ie, to death). The dedication was only effective, however, if Decius were slain among the enemy, so he had to throw himself into their ranks, and once he was killed the gods would claim both him and the enemy army. In the tapestries we see: (1) Decius bidding farewell; (2) Decius consulting the augurs; (3) Decius addressing the troops and dedicating himself as the sacrificial victim; (4) the death in battle of Decius (on the end wall); and (5) Decius's ashes are carried from the temple in a miniature urn. The theme of personal sacrifice for the public good is one that would have appealed to the first duke of Ormonde, who brought these tapestries to Kilkenny.

The collection of family pictures is impressive. Indeed it is probably fair to describe it as the finest in Ireland, although it is but a shadow of the original collection, which was dispersed after 1935. In 1900 there were 184 pictures in this room, whereas today there are only forty-nine. Historically, the two most important pictures in the collection, both of Black Tom (the nickname alluded to his hair colouring), the tenth earl of Ormond (1546–1614), are now to be found in Preston Art Gallery, Lancashire, and in a private collection in Belgium. It is hoped, however, that one day these pictures may return home to the castle.

The gallery was designed as a showpiece to impress guests and members of the public (who were admitted, as we are today, on payment of a fee), and it was used to control the image that visitors would have of the family. Visitors were meant to be impressed by the grandeur of the collection reflecting, on the one hand, the Butler family's noble lineage while, on the other, demonstrating the family's political correctness and fitness to rule. Paradoxically, the message from the gallery today is precisely the opposite. Without a guidebook, few people can read the political and religious messages that were considered of essential importance at the time the pictures were painted. The Order of the Garter or the Order of St Patrick, the presence of a crucifix, a crown or a mitre, are more puzzling than informative. The wearing of colourful robes, of armour or dark clothes – so significant to contemporaries – is just so much fancy dress to our eyes. It is still difficult not to be impressed by the gallery, but as we gaze at the pictures we see not our rulers and betters but a collection of people related to one another across time. What strikes us is the way in which the same nose, forehead or jawline tends to resurface across the generations. But, if we take the time to examine the pictures more closely, we discover that the collection includes individuals with diametrically opposed political and religious views, black sheep and white sheep, friends as well as opponents. If there is a lesson to take away from the gallery it is that human bonds endure while political and religious doctrines, like all fashions, fade away.

On the long east wall the gallery is dominated by a series of full-length paintings and the poses, particularly of the men, reflect their authority, grandeur and power. The core of the collection belongs to the late seventeenth century and many of the pictures were painted by the fashionable portraitists of the day. These include Sir Peter Lely (1618–1680), the most famous artist at the court of Charles II; Willem Wissing (1656–1687), the favourite painter of James II; Sir Godfrey Kneller (1646–1723), principal painter to William of Orange; and Michael Dahl (1656–1743), the Swedish artist who was patronised by Queen Anne. The collection is best explained under three headings: (a) the portraits assembled by the first and second dukes of Ormonde in the late seventeenth century, (b) the portraits acquired when the Butlers of Kilcash came to live in the castle in the mid-eighteenth century, and (c) the nineteenth-century pictures.

(a) Late seventeenth-century portraits

After his return in 1662, the first duke employed James Gandy (1619–1689) to copy several of Sir Anthony Van Dyck's portraits, which were already famous for the manner in which they glamorised the court of Charles I. Gandy was a pupil of Van Dyck and is important in art history terms because he was one of the first English-born painters to make a professional living as an artist, although he did almost all of his work in Ireland. His copy of the Stuart children has already been noted. In this room he is probably responsible for the half-length portrait of Thomas Wentworth and perhaps for the portrait, above the entrance door, of Elizabeth Preston (1615–1684), the wife of the first duke, together with her son, Thomas, Lord Ossory.

The oldest figure in the collection is **Helen, Lady Thurles (1588–1673)**, daughter of Sir John Poyntz of Iron Acton in Gloucestershire, and mother of the first duke. She married Thomas Butler, Lord Thurles, before 1610, in what seems to have been a love-match because his father was vehemently opposed to the wedding. Thomas drowned in 1619 while en route to England, and in this portrait Lady Thurles is shown as a widow, dressed in black and holding a veil. The portrait is by John Michael Wright (1617–1694), one of Lely's rivals as a portraitist, who is noted for the honest, unglamorous depiction of his sitters. It was painted posthumously, with the face being copied from an older portrait. Lady Thurles survived a second husband, she outmanoeuvred the Cromwellian order transporting her to Connacht and she lived to see her son become the most powerful man in Ireland. She is shown here in middle age, but in her face one can still detect the 'mien of a lady of wit and spirit', which impressed Thomas Wentworth when he met her in 1637.

The portrait of **Thomas Wentworth, (1593–1641), earl of Strafford,** was preserved in the collection because he was instrumental in transforming the Butlers from a minor aristocratic family of provincial significance into a house with an international reputation. Wentworth arrived in Dublin as lord deputy of Ireland in 1633, and for the next seven years he devoted himself to reforming the country's political structure. His administration confounded those used to a political culture of clientship, favouritism and back-scratching (it has a long history in Ireland), by completely disregarding all private interests and endeavouring to establish, for the good of the community, as he saw it, royal power as the embodiment of the State. In the struggle that was about to break out between Charles I and his parliament, Wentworth was firmly on the side of the king, believing that kingship (which to him was the same as the State) should be assisted, but not controlled, by parliament. His efficiency merged, as efficiency often does, with expediency, and he made many enemies who were on hand to bring him down when he was charged with treason in 1641. This charge arose largely because he had reportedly threatened to bring an Irish army into England so as to put down parliament and keep England loyal to the Crown. Foreshadowing what was to happen to Charles I eight years later, parliament had Wentworth tried and he was executed in May 1641. Wentworth was a complex, able, if arrogant man, and even in this somewhat idealised version of the Van Dyck original, one can sense the truth of Lady Essex Cheeke's remark that Wentworth would not keep a bodyguard, 'knowing that he has terror enough in his bended brows to amaze the apprentices'.

The portrait of **James Butler (1610–1688), the first duke of Ormonde**, was painted by John Michael Wright in 1680 or shortly afterwards. He stands on a patterned carpet, dressed in the ceremonial robes of the Order of the Garter, with his right leg protruding, displaying the garter tied just below the knee, while to his right is a draped table with the plumed hat of the Order upon it.

James Butler, the first duke of Ormonde, was the ablest member of the family. After his father drowned in 1619, his mother brought him to England and placed him with a Catholic tutor. This development did not please the English court, which demanded a mainstream, reformed education for the heir to one of Ireland's largest estates. Accordingly, he was removed from his mother's care, made a ward of court and brought up in the Protestant faith by George Abbot, Archbishop of Canterbury. Although his schooling is said to have been meagre, Abbot, or his instructors, must have been charismatic because, although Ormonde's mother, father and brother lived and died as Catholics, Ormonde himself remained faithful throughout his life to his Protestant beliefs. His first success was marriage, in 1629, to Elizabeth Preston, thereby reuniting the Ormond title with the Ormond lands. These had been divided on the death of his great grandfather, Black Tom, tenth earl of Ormond (d.1614), when the lands had gone to the earl's daughter, while the title moved sideways to the next male heir. In 1632, James succeeded to the earldoms of Ormond and Ossory and two years later he was summoned to attend Wentworth's first Irish parliament. Wentworth, fearing scenes of violence, had ordered that no one should enter the house wearing a sword. Ormonde, however, refused to hand over his blade. When the usher insisted, Ormonde told him that the only way he would take his sword would be by taking it in the guts, and so he walked on and took his seat in the house, where he was the only peer to sit with a sword. Summoned by Wentworth to explain his conduct, Ormonde replied that, while he had seen Wentworth's order, he was actually obeying a higher authority because the royal writ summoning him to parliament preserved the formal legal style of previous centuries, requiring him to come *cum glaudio cinctus*, 'girdled with a sword'. Impressed, or amused, by Ormonde's knowledge and independent spirit,

Wentworth befriended him, giving him access to court circles, which resulted in Ormonde's rapid promotion and appointment as commander-in-chief of the Irish Army at the age of thirty. In 1641, when Wentworth (by then earl of Strafford) fell from power, Ormonde defended him in the Irish House of Lords, knowing that his loyalty would cost him his position. There was clearly a bond between the two men and, before his execution, one of Wentworth's last requests to Charles I was that the position as Knight of the Garter, which his death would vacate, should be given to Ormonde. Ormonde, in fact, refused the honour, but in any event he was nominated to the Order in 1649.

After the Ulster rising of 1641, James raised the Siege of Drogheda and campaigned in Munster and Connacht. In 1642 he was created marquess of Ormonde and the story is told that it was a clerical error in the patent, whereby the clerk added the letter 'e' at the end of Ormond, which provided the spelling of the name that the family subsequently adopted. In 1643 he was appointed lord lieutenant of Ireland, but after the arrival of Cromwell he was forced to flee the country. He spent the 1650s impoverished and in exile with Charles II in France, Germany and Spain, becoming one of the king's principal confidantes and advisors. In the course of his service to the Crown he had sacrificed all of his considerable fortune and was reduced to such penury in Paris that he was forced to pawn the jewelled insignia of the Order of the Garter. After the Restoration, however, a grateful King Charles II loaded him with honours and elevated him to the dukedom of Ormonde. He was made lord high steward of the household and, in this capacity, he carried the crown at the coronation of Charles II and was present at the birth of Princess Mary (later Mary II) to authenticate the delivery. He was appointed lord lieutenant of Ireland in 1661 and returned to Dublin in regal pomp the following year. He functioned as lord lieutenant until 1669, and was reappointed between 1677 and 1685. One of his last public acts was as crown-bearer at the coronation of James II in 1685, after which he retired to his English estates. He died in 1688 at Kingston Lacy in Dorset and is buried at Westminster Abbey in London.

It has been said of Ormonde that his greatest asset was not his ability but his character, and that it was the simplicity of his loyalty that kept him aloof from the sexual and political intrigue of the Restoration court. It was, of course, a loyalty that brought him enormous rewards, although Thomas Carte, his biographer, states that his losses in the king's service exceeded his gains by nearly a million pounds (several billions in today's terms). It was certainly the case that his successors never succeeded in wiping out the debts on his estate. Perhaps Gilbert Burnet (1643–1715), bishop of Salisbury, not the most impartial of writers, may be afforded the last say. The first duke was, he said, 'a man fitted in every way for court: of a graceful appearance, a lively wit, and a cheerful temper, decent even in his vices, for he always kept up the form of religion.' The duke's legacy endures. In Kilkenny, it is primarily in the remodelled castle, the Parade and Kilkenny College. At Kinsale, in County Cork, he constructed Charles Fort, the finest seventeenth-century fortress in Ireland. In Dublin he laid out the Phoenix Park, built the Royal Hospital at Kilmainham and founded the Irish College of Surgeons.

Immediately to the right of the fireplace are William of Orange and his wife, Queen Mary II, attributed to the school of Kneller. Their presence here displays more than political correctness because the Butlers married into the family of William of Orange and were instrumental in his rise from a minor Protestant prince to a serious claimant to the English throne. The key figure in this regard was **Thomas Butler (1634–1680), earl of Ossory**. The full-length portrait of Thomas by Sir Peter Lely shows him in the ornate robes of the Order of the Garter. The picture is not the top copy – the space over his left shoulder remains blank, whereas in the version at the Elvehjem Museum of the University of Wisconsin–Madison, a sea-battle is painted in this position.

Thomas Butler was the eldest son and heir of the first duke and in 1647, after his father had surrendered Dublin to the parliamentary forces, the young Thomas was transferred from Kilkenny to France for safekeeping. Like his father, he spent the 1650s in exile, but travelled to Holland, where he met, and in 1659 married, Amelia de Nassau, a cousin of the then nine year-old prince, William of Orange. When William visited England in 1670–1671, he was accompanied by Thomas and they formed a friendship that endured despite the outbreak of war between Britain and the Netherlands. Thomas distinguished himself as a naval officer in that war. In 1672, he captained the *Victory* at the Battle of Southwold Bay, the principal English naval success of the war, and until the 1930s the gallery possessed a set of six sea pictures depicting various stages of that battle. They are now in the Royal Maritime Museum at Greenwich in England. In 1674, at the conclusion of the war (which was effectively a draw), he was chosen, because of his family connection, to convey the offer of marriage with Princess Mary, the niece of Charles II, to William of Orange. The marriage was solemnised in 1677 and it laid the foundation for William's intervention in England's affairs eleven years later.

Thomas remained in Holland and fought with William against the French at Charleroi (1677) and Mons (1678), which resulted in the independence of the United Provinces of the Netherlands. By 1680, Thomas was a leader of the party that favoured allying Britain with Holland, rather than France, but he contracted a fever later that year and died. The diarist John Evelyn stayed at his bedside 'till his last gasp', and wrote of him that he had deserved 'all that a sincere friend, a brave soldier, a virtuous courtier, a loyal subject, an honest man, a bountiful master, and good christian, could deserve of his prince and country'. To later generations he was known simply as 'the gallant Ossory'. His wife, Amelia de Nassau, died eight years later in 1688.

There is a half-length portrait of **James (1665–1745), second duke of Ormonde,** attributed to the school of Kneller. James was the eldest son of Thomas and Amelia, and when he succeeded to the title in 1688, the Butler fortunes had never been greater. Within thirty years, however, they had fallen to an all-time low.

James's first marriage was to the queen's niece, Lady Ann Hyde (1669–1685), portrayed here, in a picture attributed to the studio of Willem Wissing, with one hand on her lap and the other pointing towards her chest. Described by a contemporary as 'a pretty red-haired wife and one that has wit enough', she died in childbirth at the age of sixteen. James's second wife was Mary Somerset (1665–1733), a daughter of the duke of Beaufort. The poet John Dryden dedicated his *Palomon and Arcite* to Mary, and her full-length portrait by Michael Dahl is to the left of the fireplace. The second duke sided with William of Orange, fought at the Battle of the Boyne, secured Dublin and recaptured Kilkenny – all in July of 1690. He also entertained the triumphant William of Orange at the castle, and the gold fork used by the king at dinner was preserved and passed on like a sacred relic from generation to generation.

In January 1691 he accompanied William of Orange to The Hague, when Louis XIV, king of France, tried to reverse the decisions of the Boyne (1690) and Aughrim (1691) by threatening the Netherlands with invasion. Ormonde fought with distinction at Steenkirk in 1692 and was captured at the Battle of Neerwinden (Landen) in 1693. The English historian Thomas Babington Macaulay (1800–1859) recounts the story of how Ormonde was struck down in the battle and would have been killed but for the fact that a French guard noticed a large diamond ring on the duke's finger and concluded that he might be a valuable prisoner. After the battle he was exchanged for the duke of Berwick, a natural son of James II. Patrick Sarsfield, earl of Lucan, famous for his defence of Limerick in 1690–1691, was killed in the Battle of Neerwinden (Landen) and his wife, Honora Burke, subsequently married the duke of Berwick. Honora was the sister of Margaret Butler (née Burke) of Kilcash, and the portrait of the duchess of Berwick came to the castle in the 1760s with the Kilcash pictures.

In 1702, Ormonde was one of the small family group present at the king's bedside when William of Orange lay dying. After William's death, he went on to command the troops on the sea expedition sent against Cadiz at the commencement of the War of the Spanish Succession (1702–1713). In 1712, when the British government decided that it could no longer afford the expense and casualties of that war, Ormonde replaced the costly, but effective, duke of Marlborough as commander-in-chief and captain-general of the British armies in Flanders (then the Spanish Netherlands). He was instructed to do nothing while peace terms were being negotiated and, as a result of his inaction, Dutch and Austrian forces were defeated by the French. After the conclusion of the war he was scapegoated, deprived of the office of commander-in-chief and charged with treason. He panicked and fled to France, where he embraced the Jacobite cause, lending his support to James Francis Edward Stuart (the so-called James III), the exiled son of James II, known to posterity as the Old Pretender. Ormonde travelled to Spain, Italy and Russia before settling at Avignon, in the south of France, where he died in 1745. Three years earlier he had been visited there by the traveller Lady Mary Wortley Montagu, who wrote that he 'lives in great magnificence, is quite inoffensive, and seems to have forgot every part of his past life, and to be of no party'.

After his death, his body was embalmed and transported to England, where he was buried beside his wife and family in the Chapel of Henry VII at Westminster Abbey. To the Williamite agent, John Macky, he was 'one of the most generous, princely, brave men that ever was, good-natured to a fault; [he] loves glory and consequently is crowded with flatterers; [he] has all the qualities of a great man, except that one of a statesman, hating business'.

While the second duke was in exile, his estates were bought in 1721 by his brother, Charles, earl of Arran (1671–1758), whose three-quarter-length portrait shows him in armour, wearing a blue coat. The act of attainder, charging the second duke with treason, applied only in England, so while his Irish lands were forfeited, his Irish titles were not affected. Arran preferred to keep a low profile and never claimed the dukedom, but when he died in 1758 the titles of duke and marquess died with him because he had no son.

(b) The Kilcash Pictures

Charles, earl of Arran, settled the Butler estates on the heir-male to the title of earl of Ormonde, his Catholic cousin, John Butler of Kilcash (c.1700–1766), and so it was that the Kilcash (County Tipperary) branch of the Butler family came to Kilkenny. There is no portrait of John in the collection, but his father, Thomas Butler of Kilcash (c.1665–1734) is shown, dressed in armour, with a castle in the background. A distinguished soldier, he was, like all of the Kilcash Butlers, a supporter of the Jacobite cause. He fought for James II, in the regiment of the duke of Berwick, at the Battle of the Boyne and at the Battle of Aughrim.

John Butler of Kilcash refused to live in the castle or to claim the title, so it was his successor, Walter Butler (1703–1783), who moved to Kilkenny in 1766 – a departure lamented in the famous Irish poem on Kilcash, 'Cad a dhéanfaimid feasta gan adhmad' ('What shall we do without timber'). Walter is portrayed seated, with a spaniel, wearing a blue coat and a brown waistcoat; the classical temple and pavilion in the background may allude to the building works that he carried out in the castle demesne. Thomas Hudson's portrait of Walter's wife, Eleanor Morres (1711–1794), depicts her seated, holding a King Charles spaniel in her lap. She wears a white gown with a pink rose and a blue shawl over her shoulders. Hudson is largely remembered today because he taught Sir Joshua Reynolds for two years and painted portraits of George Frideric Handel and George II.

Another member of the Kilcash Butlers is Christopher (1673–1757), the Catholic archbishop of Cashel, County Tipperary.

The remains of Kilcash Castle, County Tipperary, home of one of the principal branches of the Butler family.

In the three-quarter-length portrait by James Latham, the 'Irish Van Dyke', the archbishop is shown seated, holding his pectoral cross (a crucifix indicating his Catholicism), with a mitre, signifying the office of bishop, on the table beside him. Christopher was a grand-nephew of the first duke and an uncle of John Butler of Kilcash. He was educated in England, at the Sorbonne, in Paris, and in Rome, where he was consecrated archbishop of Cashel in 1712. He returned to Ireland and ministered contrary to the provisions of the Penal Laws. He was responsible for developing Thurles, instead of Cashel, as the Catholic diocesan cathedral, but he himself maintained no fixed residence, moving instead from one Butler residence to another, sometimes with the authorities in hot pursuit.

One surprising picture in the collection, because it appears to be so politically incorrect, is the portrait to the left of the fireplace of **James Francis Edward Stuart (1688–1766), the Old Pretender**, shown in armour, with a crown on the table next to him. Eighteenth-century Irish society was deeply divided between those who supported William of Orange and his successors (Williamites), and those who supported the descendants of James II (Jacobites). The Williamites were Protestant, they controlled Ireland and epitomised what was subsequently called the Anglo-Irish ascendancy. The Jacobites were Catholic, disadvantaged by the Penal Laws and tended to be impoverished, or in exile, or both. This portrait is politically incorrect because it is a subversive, anti-ascendancy, Catholic icon, enshrined in what should have been a bastion of ascendancy good taste. It came to Kilkenny Castle with the Butlers of Kilcash, themselves Catholics and Jacobite supporters. Its presence in the collection, like the portraits of the duchess of Berwick and the Catholic archbishop of Cashel, serves as a reminder that the past was not as black and white as we in the present tend to think it was. The portraits reflect that the family, like many others, tried to serve two masters, swaying back and forth between what to us are opposite poles. An individual like the second duke had no compunction about being an influential court intimate one day and dying in exile the next. Eighteenth-century attitudes were different from modern ones. The portraits reflect an aristocratic society in which honour and nobility of birth were prized more highly than political or religious affiliations. Achievement and distinction, in whatever field, were respected, while the family saw itself as embracing diversity of opinion and exemplifying the dictum that blood is thicker than water.

(c) The nineteenth-century portraits

Walter's son, John, converted to Protestantism in 1764 and shortly afterwards he married Anne Wandesford, daughter and sole heiress of Earl Wandesford, the fabulously wealthy owner of the coal mines at Castlecomer, County Kilkenny. Earl Wandesford is the subject of a three-quarter-length portrait, thought to derive from the studio of Sir Joshua Reynolds, while Anne is shown seated, with her arms crossed and one glove removed. The full-length portrait of their eldest son, Walter (1770–1820), the eighteenth earl, is attributed to Sir William Beechey, portrait painter to Queen Charlotte, wife of George III.

Walter was a companion of the Prince Regent and dissipated much of the newly found family wealth maintaining himself at the fashionable haunts of London, Brighton and Bath. His influence with the prince secured him a marquessate, but his extravagance forced him to sell back to the Crown the family's right to the Prisage of Wine. There is now no portrait of Walter's wife, Anna Maria Catherine Clarke, but there are two of her relations, Sir Gilbert Clarke, painted by Kneller, and Mrs Mary Clarke, seated, wearing a yellow dress, painted by an unknown artist. Walter died childless in 1820 and was succeeded by his brother, James (1775–1838), whose portrait by John Saunders shows him as a young man. In a second portrait, by Richard Rothwell, he is shown wearing the Order of St Patrick, the principal Irish order of chivalry. The marquessate, which had died with his brother, Walter, was recreated for him, and he officiated as Chief Butler of Ireland at the coronation of George IV in 1820 – the last of the Ormondes to do so. John Saunders was a fashionable society portraitist at Bath and he also painted the picture of James Butler's wife, Grace Louisa Staples (1779–1860), which shows her as a young woman. Technically, the marquessate had died with Walter, but it was recreated again (for the third time) in 1825.

The portrait of John, the second marquess of Ormonde (1808–1854), painted by Henry Weigall, is near the entrance end of the gallery. His head is tilted slightly, he wears the star, blue sash and cloak of the Order of St Patrick, and his right hand rests on a dress sword. In the background is a table with a book and documents, testifying to his literary interests.

The most scholarly of the Ormondes, he published a life of St Canice, entitled *Vita Sancti Kannechi*, in 1853, and opened up the family archive to scholarly study. The editions of the family archive prepared by the English and Irish Manuscripts Commissions, often providing only summaries of the documents, run to eighteen volumes and these do not include all of the papers in the collection. In 1849, John played a key role in the formation of the Kilkenny Archaeological Society, which still functions as the Royal Society of Antiquaries of Ireland.

The artist Richard Buckner, a portrait painter patronised by both Queen Victoria and Prince Albert, painted the portrait of John's wife, Frances Jane Paget (1817–1903). She is seated, in a black dress, holding their son, James, in a conventional pose – she looks serene while the child looks uncomfortable and points, with outstretched hand, towards his father. Frances's father, General Sir Edward Paget (1775–1849) is shown seated, wearing a red sash.

On the left of the fireplace, near the centre of the room, is James (1844–1919), the boy on his mother's knee in the earlier picture, now third marquess of Ormonde. He is depicted in military uniform as a captain in the First Life Guards, with whom he served from 1863 until 1873. Beside him, dressed in white, is his wife, Elizabeth Harriet Grosvenor (1856–1921); both portraits are by Henry Richard Graves, a London-based portraitist.

Downstairs from the picture gallery are the kitchens, where you can get an idea of what life was like for those who lived below stairs. If you visit between April and September, you can relax with a cup of tea and a snack. En route to the kitchens you will pass some of the servants' rooms, which have been transformed into an exhibition space, generally used to display contemporary works of art.

KILKENNY CASTLE GARDENS AND DEMESNE

At the height of their power in the sixteenth and seventeenth centuries, the Butlers owned or controlled over two million acres in counties Kilkenny and Tipperary. Samuel Pepys was not far wrong when he wrote of the first duke of Ormonde, 'he is the greatest subject of any prince in Christendom, and has more acres of land than any'. By 1800 the estate had decreased, as a result of sales and forfeitures, to 25,000 acres, and by the end of the nineteenth century it was further reduced by the Land Acts to 5,000 acres, over two-thirds of which comprised mountain and woodland near Kilcash, on the slopes of Slievenamon in County Tipperary. In 1967 when Arthur, the sixth marquess, presented the castle to the town, only fifteen acres remained. A few years later the marquess bought back another fifty acres of parkland and also presented it to the townspeople so that the integrity of the castle and its nineteenth-century demesne could be maintained. This was not only generous and far-sighted, but it is likely that if he had not done it the parkland would have been developed, like every other available piece of ground in Kilkenny, for hotels, apartments and housing estates.

The present layout of the parkland and gardens is largely the work of Ninian Niven (1799–1879), a noted Victorian gardener and director of the Botanic Gardens at Glasnevin in Dublin between 1834 and 1838. What survives, however, is only a fragment because the castle gardens on which Niven spent most of his time lay to the west of Castle Road and were converted into a housing estate in the 1950s. Nonetheless, thanks to Lord Ormonde, there are sixty-five acres to enjoy, and if the weather is fine the parkland is an ideal place in which to have a picnic. Among the trees are Florencecourt yews, cut-leafed and evergreen oaks, catalpa trees, auricarias, cedars, Japanese maples and cypresses.

A short distance south of the castle is the family cemetery, where the third, fifth, sixth and seventh marquesses and their wives are

The north or garden front of Kilkenny Castle.

buried. The memorial that most visitors remember, however, lies just outside the railings of the cemetery. It commemorates the third marchioness's dog, Sandy, 'the most devoted and beloved little friend and companion', brought as near to his mistress, Elizabeth Harriet Grosvenor, in death as conventional good taste would allow. No child would disagree with the sentiment of the inscription:

> **There are men both good and true who hold that in a future state, dumb creatures we have cherished here below shall give us joyous greeting when we pass the golden gate. Oh! how earnestly I hope it may be so.**

Further to the south is an artificial lake, built as a reservoir in 1860–1861, from which water was pumped to the castle. The lake is fed by springs, and when the reservoir was being constructed the remains of an ancient mill were discovered. From the parkland one can also gain access to the **Canal Walk**, an attractive riverside walk that commences at St John's Bridge. It is called the Canal Walk because it runs beside the remains of an unfinished canal built between 1757 and 1761 with the intention of linking Kilkenny with Inistioge, some 20km to the south. Unfortunately, the money ran out before the canal could be completed. Part of the Canal Walk adjoining the castle parkland has been laid out as a sculpture park, and it has several interesting examples of modern sculpture that are well worth a visit.

There has been a garden on the north side of the castle since the fourteenth century, but the terraces and fountain were created for

Millstream and well-house on the Canal Walk.

the first duke of Ormonde in the 1680s. In 1689 the second duke commissioned John Bonnier, a London statuary-maker, to copy four pieces that stood in the king's private garden in London. Two of these lead copies, *Diana* and *Hercules*, still survive and have been set on top of plinths; their original location is unknown. The gardens have been planted with roses and restored to their nineteenth-century appearance. From the fountain there is a good view of the castle's north front with its Venetian-inspired windows, inserted about 1860.

KILKENNY DESIGN CENTRE

These buildings, directly opposite the castle's entrance gate on the Parade, were constructed about 1780 as the castle's stables. In 1965 they were converted into the Kilkenny Design Workshops, formed to promote good quality design in Irish industry. When the buildings were first constructed, the arcade facing on to the Parade was blocked up to form a solid wall, except for the coach passage underneath the green cupola. The individual arches were opened as part of the 1960s' renovations and windows were inserted. The stalls for the horses were spacious and were located on the ground floor, in the position now occupied by shops. In contrast, the accommodation for the grooms was more restricted; their rooms were upstairs, where the tea shop is today. Behind the front building is a semicircular courtyard backed by a curved stable block. The windows on the first floor, looking onto this courtyard, are circular with timber frames resembling coach wheels. The large stone blocks, inscribed with letters, were salvaged from Nelson's Pillar, a monument that stood in O'Connell Street, Dublin, which was blown-up in 1966.

You can continue walking through the grounds to Butler House, which is on Patrick Street.

Kilkenny Design Centre, built originally as the stables for Kilkenny Castle.

BUTLER HOUSE AND THE CLUB HOUSE HOTEL

Butler House was built about 1780 as a dower house for the countesses of Ormonde, where they retired after the death of a husband. (A widow's dower was her lifelong share of her husband's estate.) The plasterwork is simple but attractive, and the eighteenth-century character of the building is most apparent from the garden. The house provides year-round accommodation for visitors.

Georgian period façades, Parliament Street.

Exiting onto Patrick Street, turn right, walk past the Club House Hotel and return to the Parade. The Club House Hotel was established in conjunction with the Kilkenny Hunt Club, founded in 1797, to provide accommodation and sustenance for hunt members too exhausted (or not exhausted enough) to return home. As the significance of the club declined, the hotel gradually took over the Club House and hence acquired the name.

THE PARADE

The Parade was created by the first duke of Ormonde when he demolished the east side of Castle Street in order to create a space in front of the castle that could be used for military parades and assemblies. The Bank of Ireland building, on the corner with Patrick Street, was built in 1870. Immediately to the south is a low building, on the site of the former Kilkenny Private Theatre, which was built in 1853 as the Atheneum Club and Assembly Rooms. The Kilkenny Private Theatre was built in 1805 to stage the productions of gentleman players. Between 1805 and 1817, the theatre season was one of the highlights of the Irish social calendar. Edmund Kean (1787–1833) performed on its stage and the poet Thomas Moore (1779–1852) met his wife here.

SHEE ALMSHOUSE

Sir Richard Shee (d.1609) made a fortune from speculating in former church properties that had come on the market as a result of the Reformation. Moved by the plight of the poor, and perhaps in an effort to insure himself against hellfire, he established this almshouse in 1582. He stipulated that it should house six 'honest, poor, unmarried men' and six widows of fifty years of age or more. The men were housed on the first floor, the women on the ground floor – the provision of separate entrances, one at the front, the other at the rear, meant that there could be no accidental encounters between them. Each individual had a private room and no connection, not even conversation, was permitted between men and women. The only time they came together was for two hours of prayer, in which they were led and supervised by the master. The marriage of a resident, or refusal to attend weekly Divine Service, or conviction for an offence such as fornication, adultery or drunkenness, led to automatic expulsion.

Shee Almshouse.

The building was constructed in Tudor style and was restored in 1986. It now functions as the Kilkenny Tourist Office. The stairs that now connect the two floors would not have existed in the original structure. If you enter the building from Rose Inn Street and climb the stairs, you can exit into a narrow lane. Turn left and follow the lane to St Mary's Church.

ST MARY'S CHURCH

St Mary's was the parish church of the medieval Hightown. Although gradually reduced in size since the eighteenth century, St Mary's was a large medieval parish church, with a long chancel, an aisled nave and transepts with several side chapels, dedicated to the Holy Trinity and to SS Peter, James and Nicholas.

St Mary's Church.

By 1205 it was sufficiently well established for Hugh de Rous, bishop of Ossory (1202–1218), to convene an ecclesiastical court there. Throughout the Middle Ages, the corporation maintained the church and an annual contribution of 4d (four pennies) was collected from each house and 0.5d (a halfpenny) from each stall or shop for this purpose. The patronage and upkeep of St Mary's was a visible sign of the pride and wealth of the burgesses, its tombs and chapels reflected their status and it was an important venue for civic ritual. Both church and bell-tower, which was evidently spacious, were frequently used for meetings of the corporation and of the town court, while in the sixteenth century, if not before, it was one of the principal locations for the performance of the town plays.

Family coat of arms at St Mary's churchyard.

The wealthiest burgesses were allowed rights of burial within the church, while the remainder of the population was interred in the churchyard. The reverence with which this churchyard was viewed is evident in the ordinance of 1337, which rewarded anyone who killed pigs found within the churchyard. The churchyard and the monument room contain the finest collection of Renaissance tombs in Ireland but, regrettably, many of these have been vandalised in recent years. The church was closed to worship in 1957 and is in much need of repair.

On leaving the churchyard turn right onto High Street.

HIGH STREET

High Street, established at the end of the twelfth century, was the main thoroughfare of the medieval town. The name High Street originated in the Middle Ages when 'high' meant 'principal or main', as in the word 'highway'. It is essentially a long narrow street linking the Castle with St Canice's Cathedral. It broadens in the centre, to accommodate the medieval market place, and narrows at both ends. It is still the principal business street in Kilkenny. Many of the façades are of nineteenth- or early twentieth-century date and retain good quality lettering. Several, such as the Marble City Bar (perhaps the finest façade, with an excellent interior), were built by Parnalls of Bristol in England. Behind the façades one may occasionally glimpse the chimney or gable of a Tudor or Renaissance building.

High Street, looking towards the Tholsel.

THE THOLSEL

The name of this building, which functions as City Hall, is derived from two old English words: *toll* meaning a tax and *sael* meaning a hall. It is literally, 'the place where tolls were paid'. During the Middle Ages the Tholsel had several functions – it was the guildhall and meeting place for merchants and also a customhouse and a courthouse. The medieval Tholsel was located closer to the Parade, on the site of the present Allied Irish Bank, but it was moved to the current site shortly before 1579. The present building was constructed between 1759 and 1761. The open arcaded space on the ground floor was used into the twentieth century as a place where fresh milk and dairy products were sold. On the first floor is the assembly room, which is still used for meetings of the town corporation. The coat of arms of Kilkenny is prominently displayed on the south wall of the building.

THE MARKET CROSS

The market cross of the medieval town was located in the High Street, immediately to the north of the Tholsel. The cross was a

canopied structure set on top of a stepped base. Erected in 1335, it was removed in 1771 with the intention of being rebuilt at the Parade. Instead, the stonework vanished – almost certainly into the foundations of a contemporary building project. Only drawings survive of the cross, which was the finest in medieval Ireland. I feel sure that, one of these days, the stones will resurface when a house of the period is being renovated or rebuilt.

The market cross of Kilkenny, as depicted in a now lost painting of about 1760.

THE BUTTER SLIP

Just north of the Tholsel is the Butter Slip, a narrow passage linking High Street with St Kieran's Street. It derives its name from the fact that women traditionally came here to sell butter. The buildings on either side were constructed in the early years of the seventeenth century and still retain attractive stone window jambs and doorways. One of them, functioning now as Pordello's Restaurant, has several *in situ* roof- and floor-timbers from the period.

Continue down the Butter Slip to the foot of the steps and turn left onto St Kieran's Street; a short walk will bring you to Kyteler's Inn.

The Butter Slip.

KYTELER'S INN

Although first referred to in 1432, this house is traditionally associated with Alice Kyteler, tried for witchcraft and heresy in 1324. In the Middle Ages, the word 'inn' was interchangeable with 'residence', but there is no evidence that the house was used for lodging guests. The earliest parts of the present building (the twin-light window in the north wall) may be of early fourteenth-century date. The vaulted

Kyteler's Inn.

chamber, or undercroft, downstairs dates to the late fifteenth or sixteenth century, while the superstructure, with its prominent door and tall windows, belongs to the eighteenth century. At the rear is St Kieran's Well, first mentioned in 1207. The origin of the name 'St Kieran's Well' is unknown – it probably functioned as the Kyteler's source of drinking water. Continue on from St Kieran Street to Parliament Street.

SITE OF THE PARLIAMENT HOUSE OF THE CONFEDERATION OF KILKENNY, 1642

Nothing now survives of the building in which the Confederation of Kilkenny first assembled in 1642. This was one of Robert Shee's town houses, built by his grandfather, Sir Richard Shee (d.1609). It was a

Eighteenth-century teahouse, originally built as a garden feature beside the River Nore at Bateman Quay.

substantial building, with thirty-three rooms. One of the apartments, measuring 16m by 15m, was spacious enough to function as the assembly room. The surviving remains of the house were removed in 1861 and the space was cleared to provide access to the Kilkenny Corporation Markets. In the 1980s, this access route was turned into a street linking Parliament Street with St John's Bridge. A plaque marks the site of the parliament house.

THE COURTHOUSE ('GRACE'S OLD CASTLE')

In 1566, James Grace, a member of a local gentry family, handed over this building, originally a fortified town house, to the townspeople for use as a county jail. In return, he was appointed governor of the jail and given an annual income of £6 13s 4d for life. The building was substantially rebuilt c.1790–1795, when the present classical façade was constructed. The interior is a close copy of the courthouse designed for Waterford by James Gandon (1743–1823), the architect of the Four Courts in Dublin. The balcony and steps were added about 1830.

ROTHE HOUSE

Rothe House, built by John Rothe and his wife, Rose Archer, between 1594 and 1610, is the most complete example of a Tudor merchant's house in the city, and it provides an almost unique insight into the living conditions of the wealthy urban middle class at this time. It consists of three houses, separated by courtyards and linked by side-buildings, arranged parallel to each other towards the front of a long burgage plot. Each house is rectangular in plan and rises to a height of three storeys. The first house, fronting onto the street, has an arcaded ground floor that functioned as a covered walkway linking the house to its neighbours; behind the walkway were shops with cellars underneath for storage.

Rothe House, built in 1594.

The main reception room on the first floor, heated by open fireplaces, was a spacious timber-panelled hall, with a stuccoed ceiling and a projecting (or oriel) window overlooking the street below. Rothe's private chambers were located beside this room, while the servants' quarters were situated under the roof on the second floor. The master bedroom was on the north side of the second house, while the southern two-thirds of this house comprised Rose Archer's suite of apartments, with its own service area, including a kitchen. The principal kitchen, however, occupied the ground floor of the third house, while the children's rooms (there were four sons and eight daughters) were located on the floors above. In all, spread between the three houses, there were twenty-three living rooms, allowing husband, wife and children to lead relatively separate lives. In addition there was a brew-house, a kiln, a well, a cistern and a long garden, complete with

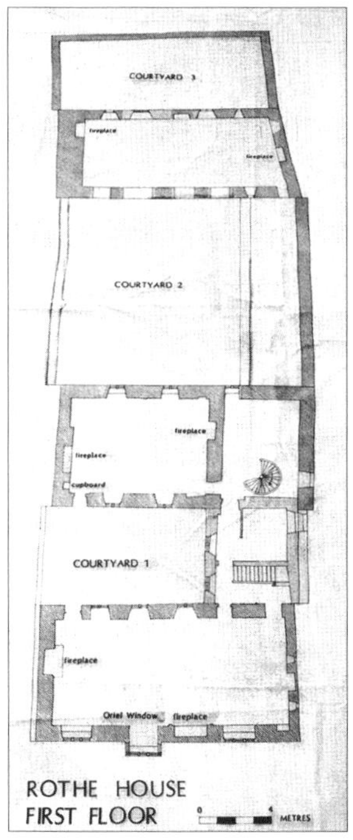

Plan of the first floor of Rothe House.

a pigeon house, which stretched back to the town wall. The garden adjoined a defensive tower on the town wall, which was converted shortly afterwards into a summerhouse for the Rothes. This complex of buildings, by no means the largest 'mansion house' in the town, was, in effect, a miniature Renaissance palazzo.

The owner of Rothe House, John Rothe, was mayor of Kilkenny in 1613, and one may note in passing that his wife was an Archer, his son-in-law a Shee. John Rothe died in 1620 and from his will it is clear that virtually all of his wealth was derived from properties throughout counties Kilkenny and Tipperary. With only two exceptions, all were former church lands. Indeed, Rothe House itself was built on property that, for at least 150 years, had been the town house of the Cistercian abbots of Duiske Abbey, Graiguenamanagh. Like other members of their class, the Rothes may have been devoutly Catholic, but their wealth and social position were based on the disestablishment of the Catholic Church.

John Rothe's will also provides an insight into the furnishings of such buildings. It mentions dining tables, extendible tables, chairs, benches, stools, long stools, joint-stools (ie, crafted by a joiner), cupboards, linen cupboards, a great cypress chest, a cypress bureau, keyboard instruments; tablecloths and coverings of linen, diaper-linen and the linen known as Holland cloth; canopied beds with sea-green curtains, tapestry coverlets, mattresses of feathers and flocks; vessels and utensils of silver, pewter, brass, hammered metal ('batry') and iron; and jewels of gold and silver. The living

Courtyard, Rothe House.

standards of the urban bourgeoisie undoubtedly improved during the late sixteenth century, but it is interesting to note that there was no change in conditions for the poor. The wages paid to labourers in 1603, for instance, were virtually identical to those paid in 1349.

The Kilkenny Archaeological Society's museum in Rothe House. This room was formerly the servants' quarters.

Dispossessed in 1654 by the Cromwellian Order of Confiscation, the Rothes regained this property after the Restoration in 1660. The family sided with James II at the Battle of the Boyne, however, lost everything and emigrated to France, where they established a Rothe regiment in the French Army. The house functions today as the headquarters and museum of the Kilkenny Archaeological Society. None of the original furnishings survive and the visitor has to exercise their imagination in order to visualise the splendour of the house in Elizabethan times.

ST FRANCIS'S ABBEY

The Franciscan Friary occupied a one-hectare precinct located on the northeastern corner of Hightown, bounded on the north by the River Bregagh and on the east by the River Nore. The site is low-lying, on soft alluvial soil that was subject, until recent drainage measures, to severe winter flooding. The founder appears to have been Richard Marshall, lord of Kilkenny from 1231 to 1234, although the first definite reference to the Franciscans at Kilkenny does not occur until 1245.

The surviving remains consist of the thirteenth-century choir, with an east end added in the 1320s, and a belfry, commenced in the 1340s but apparently left unfinished until the fifteenth century because of the impact of the Black Death. The most famous member of the community was Friar John Clyn, Ireland's principal fourteenth-century chronicler.

A note of caution: the building lies within the Smithwick's (now Guinness's) Brewery complex and the security men on the gate tend to be officious and somewhat jittery with unannounced visitors. If you have a particular wish to visit the ruin itself rather than view it from the lane outside, it is advisable to ring the Brewery in advance and make an appointment.

ST CANICE'S CATHEDRAL

The English word 'cathedral' is derived from the Latin word *cathedra*, meaning a chair, a cathedral being the place where the bishop has his seat. From the time of the reorganisation of the Irish Church at the Synod of Ráith Bressail in 1111, which was held near Cashel, County Tipperary, St Canice's has been the cathedral of the diocese of Ossory – the seat of the bishops of Ossory. The tradition of Christian

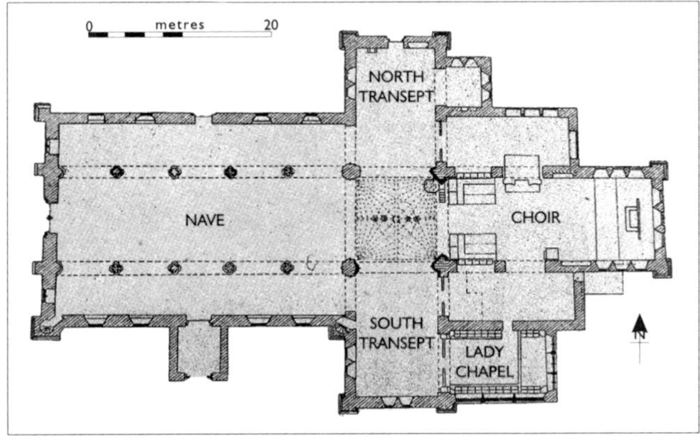

Plan of St Canice's Cathedral.

worship on this site probably goes back to the sixth or seventh century, when the cult of St Canice was first introduced. The present building, however, was not the first one on the site.

A cathedral was built in Romanesque style (characterised by rounded arches and round-headed windows) during the twelfth century, and some carved fragments from this church are preserved in the north aisle. A carved fragment from the Romanesque church can also be seen built into the external south wall of the south transept, just opposite the round tower. Restoration work in the nineteenth century discovered what may be the remains of a pre-Romanesque church in the area of the north transept.

The impressive interior of St Canice's Cathedral.

The present building was commenced shortly after the appointment of the diocese's first Anglo-Norman bishop, Hugh de Rous (bishop of Ossory, 1202–1218). Just as in England, where the victorious Normans built huge cathedrals to impress the conquered English, one of the first projects initiated by the Anglo-Normans in Ireland was the construction of large cathedrals so as to overawe the defeated Irish. The cathedral was built in the new Gothic style, with its preference for pointed arches and pointed-headed windows. At the east end it is obvious that the cathedral was commenced during a transitional stage because both round-headed and pointed-headed windows were used together. The east end, consisting of the choir and transepts, seems to have been built by about 1230. Work then stopped for about a decade until the nave was built between the 1240s and 1260s. Finally, during the 1280s, the Lady Chapel (a chapel dedicated to the Blessed Virgin Mary) was added. The building is one of the most attractive medieval churches in Ireland and still preserves the unity of its thirteenth-century design.

On Friday, 22 May 1332, Friar Clyn tells us that 'the belfry and a great part of the choir of St Canice's, Kilkenny, collapsed, demolishing the entrance to the side chapels, the bells and the timber work, a most terrible and pitiful sight to behold'. The collapse probably resulted from the punishment inflicted on William Outlaw, Alice Kyteler's son, after the heresy trial of 1324. Having been found guilty, Outlaw repented and was granted forgiveness on condition that he paid for the cost of re-roofing the cathedral's choir with lead. It is thought that the weight of the new lead was too great and that it brought down both the choir and the tower. The damaged parts were rebuilt in the 1350s by Bishop Richard de Ledrede, but it was not until about 1460 that the beautiful vault (a lierne vault) over the roof-crossing was constructed. After the Cromwellian capture of the city in 1650, the cathedral was vandalised and looted. On his return to Kilkenny after the Restoration, Griffith Williams, the Church of Ireland bishop of Ossory from 1641 to 1672, described its condition:

> The great, and famous, most beautiful cathedral church of saint Keney, they [the Cromwellians] have utterly defaced, and ruined, thrown down all the Roof of it, taken away five great and goodly Bells, broken down all the windows, and carried away every bit of the Glass, that they say was worth a very great deal; and all the doors of it that Hogs might come, and root, and Dogs gnaw the Bones of the dead .... and they brake down a most exquisite Marble Font (wherein the Christian's Children were regenerated) all to pieces, and threw down the many *many* goodly Marble Monuments, that were theirein, and especially that stately and costly Monument of the most honourable and noble Family of the House of Ormond, and divers others ...

Bishop Williams commenced the task of repairing the church and appears to have completed it by 1672. Further work was carried out by Bishop Richard Pococke (1704–1765) between 1756 and 1763, and a list of subscribers to that restoration is to be found on a wall in the north transept. It is of interest to note, in passing, that Pococke's successor as bishop of Ossory was Charles Dodgson, the grandfather of Lewis Carroll, author of *Alice in Wonderland*. The present appearance of the cathedral is due to the restoration work carried out between 1863 and 1870, when all plaster was removed from the internal walls. The unimpeded view from end to end was also created at this time and the hammer-beam roof was added to the nave and the transepts.

As the largest church in medieval Kilkenny, the cathedral was the setting for imposing ceremonies on major feast days, such as Palm Sunday and Easter Sunday, when the sovereign and corporation of Hightown were expected to attend. Such occasions could be fractious and sometimes intensified the rivalry that existed between Irishtown and Hightown. The surviving burial monuments reflect a patronage that was derived, until the sixteenth century, from the Irishtown elite. The thirteenth- and fourteenth-century tombs commemorate ecclesiastics, principally bishops and cathedral canons, and the occasional prominent lay-person. During the sixteenth century, however, the cathedral became a regional showpiece as the principal burial place of the earls of Ormond and of other important landowners in the Kilkenny area, such as the Graces, lords of Courtstown, the Shortals, lords of Ballylarkin and the Purcells of Foulksrath.

Stone image of a sixteenth-century abbess. It is inserted into the wall of the sexton's house beside St Canice's Cathedral.

The medieval tombs

There are eighty-one medieval funerary monuments in the cathedral, ranging in date from the thirteenth to the sixteenth century. Thirty-three have inscriptions providing a date: two in the thirteenth century, two in the fourteenth century and twenty-nine in the sixteenth century. Other monuments can be dated on the basis of their style. The absence of inscriptions is due to two reasons. Firstly, for a time during the Middle Ages it was believed to be vain (ie, sinful) to place an individual's name on a tomb; secondly, some tombs may have had painted inscriptions that have worn away over time.

Side panel from a sixteenth-century tomb at St Canice's Cathedral. It was customary to place images of saints on tombs in the hope that they would intercede with God on behalf of the deceased. Not all of the saints on this panel can be identified, but St Catherine of Alexandria can be distinguished with the sword and wheel on which, according to legend, she was tortured.

The tombs provide a useful insight into the social history of medieval Kilkenny. The magnificence or simplicity of the tombs reflected the social hierarchy of life continuing into death. The nobles and gentry, such as the Butlers, Graces and Shortals, are depicted in splendid attire on elaborate effigial tombs; the merchant families of Kilkenny are commemorated by floor slabs, some with delicately interlaced crosses, others with a simpler combination of spiritual motifs. There are no memorials to artisans, labourers or peasants – they simply could not afford the cost of commissioning a tomb.

The best-known and most beautiful tomb in the cathedral is the double effigy monument of Piers Butler, eighth earl of Ormond (d. 1539) and his wife, Margaret FitzGerald (d.1542), which is in the south transept; its original location is unknown. It was placed here in 1854 by James, second marquess of Ormonde, who gathered together the fragments of the various Butler monuments and reassembled them in the south transept. Piers Butler is dressed in typical Irish armour of the early sixteenth century. Although it is a style that was out of fashion in Britain and the Continent, it was perfectly suited to the guerrilla warfare that characterised Ireland, where battles were rarely set-piece engagements. Margaret FitzGerald is dressed in a long flowing gown that reaches down to her toes. It is belted high on the waist, and the long ornamental belt falls down the front of her robe. On her head she wears a heart-shaped (or horned) headdress, attached to which is a veil that falls to her shoulders. On either side of her neck little angels are portrayed holding the veil. The sides of the tomb are not the originals. The north side is carved with six apostles: St Philip (holding the loaves); St Andrew (book and saltire cross); St Simon (axe and book); St Thaddeus (club and book); St James of Compostela, identified by his scallop shells; and St Matthew (a sword). The south side is carved with the figure of Christ bound to a pillar, the emblems of the Passion and Crucifixion, and two shields, one bearing the Butler arms, the other the arms of the Cantwells, indicating that it originally belonged to a different tomb.

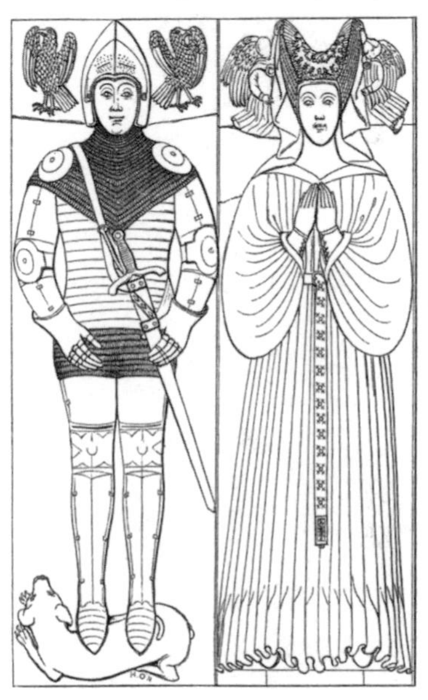

Double effigy tomb of Piers Butler (d.1539), eighth earl of Ormond, and his wife, Margaret FitzGerald (d.1542), in the south transept of St Canice's Cathedral.

Head-slab of a man, dating to the early fourteenth century, St Canice's Cathedral.

Beside the tomb of Piers Butler and Margaret FitzGerald is the unidentified tomb of a Butler knight. At one time this was believed to be the tomb of Piers's successor, James Butler, ninth earl of Ormond who, with fifty others, was poisoned at a party in London in 1546 (such a death was one of the occupational hazards of being an earl). It is more likely, however, that it was erected at the same time as Piers Butler's monument, as a memorial to Piers's father.

Detail, representing the evangelist St Mark, from the choir stalls at St Canice's Cathedral.

The Choir

The five circular perforations in the lierne vaulting over the crossing were for bell ropes, which would have stretched right down to the floor. The present eight bells are rung from a loft in the tower. The choir stalls were carved from Danubian oak at Bruges, in Belguim, in 1904. The panels represent scenes from Irish history: (1) St Patrick addressing King Lóeguire and his nobles at the Hill of Tara;

(2) panels showing St Fiacc of Sletty, County Carlow, and (3) St Canice expounding Christian doctrine; (4) Strongbow and the bishop of Ossory planning to rebuild the cathedral. The floor of the sanctuary is composed of four different marbles, drawn from the four provinces of Ireland – grey from Tyrone, red from Kerry, green from Connemara, County Galway, and black from Kilkenny.

Round-headed and pointed-headed windows in the choir of St Canice's Cathedral, reflecting the transition in style from Romanesque to Gothic architecture.

In the north wall of the sanctuary is the tomb of Bishop Richard de Ledrede (bishop of Ossory, 1317–1360), dressed in a bishop's pontificals, except for his feet, which are clad in the sandals of a member of the Franciscan order. The tomb is uninscribed, but there is little doubt about the identification because de Ledrede was the only Franciscan bishop of Ossory. The tomb was reassembled in this position in 1868, when it was discovered that it fitted the niche exactly.

In the 1350s, Bishop de Ledrede filled the great east window with glass of such quality that it dazzled the papal nuncio, Archbishop Rinuccini, when he visited Kilkenny in 1645. The glass, according to Rinuccini, depicted the history of the life, passion, resurrection and ascension of Our Lord. It is said that Rinuccini offered £700 for the window, but the offer was refused. Five years later, the windows were smashed and removed by Cromwellian soldiers. The present window was erected by the third marquess of Ormonde in 1875 and depicts the same theme as the fourteenth-century original.

North transept

The medieval *cathedra* or bishop's seat has been reassembled against the north wall. This is St Kieran's Chair. Kieran (not Canice) was the patron saint of the diocese of Ossory, and according to legend the stone beneath the seat was the one on which Kieran's successors were enthroned. The stone was said to have been moved in due course from St Kieran's Church at Sierkieran, County Offaly, to Aghaboe, County Laois, and from there to Kilkenny. The sides of the chair, with the decorated arms, date to the thirteenth century. After their enthronement in the choir, the bishops of Ossory are brought into the transept and seated in this chair to symbolise the continuity of their ministry.

The nave

Notable features in the nave are the effigial tombs of John Grace (d.1552), James Shortals (d.1507), Honorina Grace (d.1596) and Richard Butler, first Viscount Mountgarret (d.1571). Among the simpler tombs there is a plain slab placed against the north wall, which has an inscription in Norman-French commemorating Jose(ph) de Kyteler, who died between 1285 and 1288. He was presumably one of Alice Kyteler's ancestors.

At the bottom of the west window is a gallery with a central pointed arch. It is thought that this was designed so that it could be occupied by a small choir on Easter Sunday when the bishop formally processes through the west door, and the view of the cathedral from this point was clearly designed to impress. Near the entrance porch is the thirteenth-century baptismal font. The design, with its fluted sides, central pier and four supporting columns, is characteristic of the Kilkenny area. The font was broken by Cromwell's soldiers and it now stands on a modern base. The cover, showing a fish – an early symbol of Christianity – was designed by Oisín Kelly, the renowned sculptor, and was made by Peter Donovan in Kilkenny in 1972. The original base was subsequently rediscovered when a grave was being dug in the churchyard and it now lies against the south wall.

The round tower

Probably constructed close to the year 1100, St Canice's round tower is the oldest building in Kilkenny. The base was excavated in 1847–1848 and it was discovered that the tower had been built on an earlier graveyard. The remains of two adults and two children were recovered. The foundations were two feet (60cm) deep. Theoretically, such a foundation on graveyard clay is inadequate, but the building has stood the test of time, probably because it is essentially a cylinder – cylinders tend to be very stable because all stress is conveyed directly to the ground. With such shallow foundations, a door at ground level would almost certainly cause the structure to collapse. The door of a round tower was placed some eight feet (2.5m) above ground level not for defensive reasons but for structural ones. The part of the tower below the door is effectively its foundation and originally it would have been filled with earth.

Common Hall Lane, approaching St Canice's Cathedral.

The tower is one hundred feet (30.2m) in height. Originally there were seven floors, together with a basement and, probably, a conical cap. The second to fifth floors are lit by one window; there is no window in the sixth floor, but the seventh floor is lit by six lintelled (or flat-headed) windows. The parapet and roof were probably added in the Middle Ages when the conical cap was removed. Internally, the tower is fitted with ladders and floors right to the top, from where there is a delightful view of the city and its environs.

Round towers were not built as lookouts or as defences from the Vikings, as popularly thought. The Irish name, *cloigtheach* (literally, 'bell-house'), indicates that their function was as belfries. Round towers are the Irish equivalent of the belfries that were constructed at the west end of Continental churches built about the same time, such as the cathedrals at Speyer in Germany or Compostela in Spain. The combination of the round-headed door and flat-headed windows indicates that the Kilkenny tower was built at a time when Romanesque influences were beginning to be adopted. This would suggest a date of around 1100, so it is possible that the tower was built to celebrate St Canice's elevation to cathedral status in 1111.

St Canice's Library

In the northwest corner of the churchyard is St Canice's Library, which was built in 1693 on the site of the grammar school founded before 1539 by Piers Butler, eighth earl of Ormond, and his wife, Margaret FitzGerald. In 1684 the grammar school was moved to the east bank of the River Nore and became known as Kilkenny College. Like most cathedral libraries the majority of the books are theological, but the library also possesses some fine examples of early printed books and an interesting collection of early bibles.

Nineteenth-century burial monument, in the form of a Celtic cross, at St Canice's Cathedral.

Irishtown defences

At the west and north ends of St Canice's churchyard is a raised embankment that has been used for burial purposes. This earthen bank is all that remains of the medieval fortifications of Irishtown. The late medieval defences of Irishtown enclosed a roughly subrectangular space, 380m by 260m in extent, with a circumference of about 600m, and occupying an area of about ten hectares (twenty-four acres). As with Hightown, there is no evidence for an eastern river wall nor for a southern, or Bregagh, wall. No wall-towers are known, but there were four gates: Dean's Gate, on the road leading west towards Tullaroan and Thurles, County Tipperary; Troy's Gate, spanning the route leading north towards Freshford and Roscrea, County Tipperary; Green's Gate, controlling access from the east across Green's Bridge; and Water Gate, at the junction with Hightown.

THE BISHOP'S PALACE

During the first half of the thirteenth century, the episcopal palace appears to have been outside the pre-Norman ecclesiastical enclosure. This was abandoned by Geoffrey St Leger, bishop of Ossory from 1260 to 1287, in preference for a new site, referred to in subsequent documents as Oldcourt. In turn, Oldcourt was deserted by Bishop Richard de Ledrede when he built *Nova Curia*, or New Court, to the

The Bishop's Robing Room,
beside St Canice's Cathedral, built in 1758.

northeast of St Canice's Cathedral. New Court, probably built during the 1350s, consisted of a fortified tower, with an adjoining hall-house, supported on a vaulted chamber or undercroft. It was substantially remodelled in 1735–1736, when it acquired its present appearance of a Georgian house.

BLACK ABBEY

The Dominican Friary is popularly known as the 'Black Abbey' because, during the Middle Ages, the Dominican friars wore a black habit. The friary was established outside the town walls c.1225 by William Marshall the Younger. The surviving remains consist of a

The Dominican Friary ('Black Abbey'), founded around 1225.
(photo: Oliver of Kilkenny)

nave with a south aisle, probably thirteenth century in date, a south transept, constructed c.1300, a crossing-tower inserted in 1527, a fifteenth-century west tower and a fragment of the cloistral buildings' west range. These form a small part of the original complex of buildings that occupied an area of almost one hectare and was bounded by a precinct wall.

Although it did not play as prominent a role in the affairs of the town as St Mary's, it enjoyed, nonetheless, a high level of favour and patronage from the corporation and the burgesses. In 1334 the

Dominicans were given the privilege of having their own keys to the town gate so that they could have access when they wished. In 1353 the corporation granted them the rent from two houses to provide bread and wine for the celebration of Masses. From 1405 the friary's chapter house, evidently one of the more spacious rooms in Kilkenny, was used for the annual election of the town's first officer – the sovereign. The surviving tombs indicate that the friars enjoyed continuous patronage from the burgesses between the thirteenth and sixteenth centuries. Within the church is a fine fifteenth-century alabaster image of the Holy Trinity. The date of 1264, which is cut into its base, is evidently bogus because Arabic numerals did not come into common use until the sixteenth century.

ST MARY'S CATHEDRAL

The Catholic Cathedral of the diocese of Ossory was built between 1843 and 1857, based on the design of the medieval English Gothic

St Mary's Cathedral.
(photo: Oliver of Kilkenny)

cathedral of Gloucester. The tower is the most conspicuous building in the city and is visible from all approaches to Kilkenny. With its spiky pinnacles, the tower has a somewhat gaunt look and its height is out of proportion to the length of the nave. It is said the reason for this disparity is that, in the aftermath of the Great Famine (1845–1849), finances were exhausted and the builders settled for an arcade of five bays rather than the intended arcade of eight bays. Internally, the sanctuary is ornately decorated with mosaics, but the rest of the building is plain. In the Cathedral Close, the presbytery was erected in 1864 and the chapter house in 1899, creating an interesting High Victorian ensemble of buildings.

THE TOWN WALLS

Near St Mary's Cathedral is one of the most interesting surviving sections of the town wall, comprising a short stretch of the curtain wall with two blocked arrow loops. These loops are long narrow slits, which opened into a space or embrasure in the thickness of the wall, in which an archer could stand. The wall is now overshadowed by apartments, which were recently constructed close to it.

The town wall, looking from the Black Abbey towards the Black Freren Gate.

During the Middle Ages, the towns of Hightown (Englishtown) and Irishtown were separately defended and administered. The defences of Hightown enclosed a roughly rectangular area, with maximum dimensions of 800m by 350m and a circumference of about 1,450m, enclosing an area of about twenty-eight hectares (seventy acres). On the north side the town wall was bounded by the River Bregagh, while on the west it hugged a ridge of high ground for much of its length before turning eastwards to link up with the castle's defences. The west wall seems to have been perceived as the most important because, with four wall-towers and two turrets, it was the most strongly fortified. The north wall was defended by a single turret at the northeast corner while, apart from the angle-tower known as 'Talbot's' Bastion (which it shared with the west wall), the south wall

'Talbot's' Bastion, at the southwest corner of the town walls, as depicted by Francis Grose in 1791.

had neither towers nor turrets, presumably because its proximity to the castle was regarded as sufficient defence. There is no evidence for the existence of a river wall beside the River Nore. The steep scarp between the castle and St John's Bridge formed a formidable natural barrier, while the absence of a wall north of St John's Bridge may be explained either because the river provided sufficient defence or because a wall would have obstructed access to quays and landing platforms.

The approach to the Dominican Friary ('Black Abbey'), through the Black Freren Gate, as it used to look before 'urban renewal' in the 1990s.

There were seven gatehouses along the course of the wall: Castle Gate, on the main road, leading southeast to Thomastown and New Ross, County Wexford; St Patrick's Gate, straddling the route leading south to Waterford; Walkin's Gate, on the road leading southwest towards Callan and Clonmel, County Tipperary; St James's Gate, on the route leading west to Cashel, County Tipperary; Black Freren (Black Friar's) Gate, perhaps no more than a postern or side entrance, giving access to the Dominican Friary; Irishtown Gate, at the junction with Irishtown; and St John's Gate, on the west side of St John's Bridge. Only a fragment of one gatehouse, the Black Freren Gate, survives.

The wall was constructed from locally quarried limestone, mostly from the Black Quarry, and it survives to a height of 4.5m in places. It would have been higher originally and topped with a crenellated wall-walk. Additional defence was provided by the presence of arrow embrasures at, or just above, ground level in the south and west walls, and arrow loops in the north wall. The wall itself averaged 1.2m to 1.4m in thickness, and there was an external fosse, or dry moat, between 4m and 5.5m wide, averaging 1.5m in depth. The initial defences were presumably of earth, although no trace of them appears to have been found during recent archaeological excavations. Their former presence is indicated by the fact that the settlement was evidently enclosed in 1207 when William Marshall, lord of Leinster, granted his charter. The surviving stone fabric is almost entirely thirteenth century in date. Although the town defences were substantially inferior in quality to those of the castle, the construction of the wall was the largest civic architectural undertaking of the medieval townspeople.

THE MEDIEVAL SUBURB OF ST JOHN'S

Throughout the Middle Ages the portion of Kilkenny situated on the east bank of the River Nore functioned as a separate suburb, with its own officials responsible for the implementation of law and order. Colloquially, the area is referred to as 'the Continent' because it lies across the water. On the east side of St John's Bridge is the Bridge House, a Tudor residence that belonged to the Ormondes and was the principal residence of the duke of Ormonde's brother, Charles Butler (1671–1758), earl of Arran, while he lived in the city. It has an attractive bow window and some fine internal plasterwork.

Bridge House, the residence of Charles Butler (1671–1758), earl of Arran.

KILKENNY COLLEGE (NOW THE COUNTY OFFICES)

Kilkenny College was the successor to the grammar school established, before 1539, beside St Canice's Cathedral by Piers Butler. It was moved to this location in 1684, and for a period of six months in 1690 it functioned as a university. The present building, a purpose-built square schoolhouse with an attractive Georgian entrance door, was constructed in 1782. It continued to function as a school until 1985, when the college sold the building and transferred to more

Jonathan Swift, a former student of Kilkenny College.

spacious premises on the outskirts of the city. The building was purchased and refurbished by Kilkenny County Council and it now functions as County Hall. Among Kilkenny College's many distinguished pupils were the historian Richard Stanihurst (1547–1618), Jonathan Swift (1667–1745), the author of *Gulliver's Travels*, the philosopher George Berkeley (1685–1753), the dramatists William Congreve (1670–1729) and George Farquahar (1678–1707) and Admiral David (later Earl) Beatty (1871–1936).

ST JOHN'S ABBEY

The first Augustinian monks to arrive in Kilkenny (probably in pre-Norman times) were placed by the bishop of Ossory beside Green's Bridge, on a hill opposite St Canice's Cathedral. In 1211 they moved to the rapidly developing suburb of St John's. The parish of St John's was created, the Augustinians were appointed to maintain it and their priory church functioned as the parish church. The monastic precinct comprised almost two hectares (five acres) and stretched along the northern side of the burgages from Michael Street to the

River Nore. The surviving remains of the church consist of the early thirteenth-century chancel and Lady Chapel, built c.1280, and known from the continuous run of its windows as 'the lantern of Ireland'. After its abandonment by the Augustinians, the site at Green's Bridge became St Maul's Chapel. The identification of Maul has posed problems, and the historian Meredith Hanmer (1543–1604), writing in the late sixteenth century, was the first to record the tradition that the patron was Maula, the mother of Canice. Although this seems implausible, no better explanation of the dedication has been proposed.

St John's Church (Church of Ireland),
incorporating parts of the medieval Augustinian Abbey of St John.

HOSPITAL OF ST MARY MAGDALEN (MAUDLIN CASTLE)

The exact foundation date of the Hospital of St Mary Magdalen, situated in Maudlin Street on the south side of the suburb of St John's, is unclear, but it was in existence by 1327. The early sixteenth-century Maudlin (the name is derived from Magdalen) Castle, a tower house, still survives, isolated now in a forest of houses, but an old engraving, based on the painting shown below, shows that it protected the entrance gate leading into the hospital enclosure. In 1352 the hospital was funded by urban rents and its master was responsible to the sovereign of Hightown. Its internal spatial arrangements are unknown, but by the sixteenth century it was the practice to keep the best chamber for the treatment of the burgesses.

View from Wind Gap by an unknown Irish artist, painted about 1770. Kilkenny Castle, St Canice's Cathedral and Maudlin Castle are all visible.

WIND GAP

The ground rises at the southern end of Maudlin Street, providing a fine view of the castle and city across the River Nore. This was a favoured spot for eighteenth- and nineteenth-century artists, and many sketches, prints and views survive of the city from this angle. Just across the road is Windgap Cottage, the home of the novelist John Banim (1798–1842), best remembered for his series of novels entitled *Tales by the O'Hara Family*. Sometimes referred to as 'Ireland's Walter Scott', Banim wrote several historical novels that provide a vivid insight into life in Kilkenny during the eighteenth and nineteenth centuries. The poverty of the community depicted by Banim, with its rigid social and religious hierarchies, its social immobility and absence of opportunity, is in sharp contrast to the modern city, with its energetic activity, vibrant social life and welcoming air.